Joshua

The Lord's Promise Fulfilled

You know in your hearts and souls, all of you, that not one word has failed of all the good things that the LORD your God has promised concerning you. All have come to pass for you; not one of them has failed.

Joshua 23:14

By Gary Dunker

CONCORDIA PUBLISHING HOUSE · SAINT LOUIS

3558 S. Jefferson Ave., St. Louis, MO 63118-3968
1-800-325-3040 • www.cph.org

By Gary Dunker

Edited by Robert C. Baker

This publication may be available in braille, in large print, or on cassette tape for the visually impaired. Please allow 8 to 12 weeks for delivery. Write to the Library for the Blind, 7550 Watson Rd., St. Louis, MO 63119-4409; call toll-free 1-888-215-2455; or visit the Web site: www.blindmission.org.

4 5 6 7 8 9 10 11 12 33 32 31 30 29 28 27 26 25

Contents

History	*Date (BC)*	*Joshua*
Hammurabi begins reign in Babylonia	1792	
Moses born in Egypt (Exodus 2:1–8)	1526	
	1510	Earliest possible date for birth of Joshua (see Joshua 24:29)
Amenhotep II becomes Pharaoh of Egypt	1450	
Exodus from Egypt (Exodus 12:31–51)	1446	
Israelites wander in the wilderness; Moses writes Pentateuch (Genesis–Deuteronomy)	1446–1406	
Construction of tabernacle (Exodus 25–30; 35–40)	1445	
Aaron dies on Mount Hor (Numbers 33:38–39) Moses dies on Mount Nebo (Deuteronomy 34)	1407/6	Joshua appointed leader after death of Moses (Deuteronomy 34:9; Joshua 1:1–9)
Israelites cross the Jordan (Joshua 4:19) First Passover in the land (Joshua 5:10)	April 1406	
	1406–1400	Joshua leads conquest of Canaan (Joshua 1–3)
	1400	Joshua gives Hebron to Caleb (Joshua 14:13)
	1399	Joshua dies (Joshua 24:29)
Amenhotep IV, "Akhenaten," father of Tutankhamen, becomes Pharaoh	1352	

An Outline of Joshua

A cursory glance of Joshua might tempt readers to conclude that this book is nothing more than a chronicle of the Israelite people. Although this sixth book of the Bible does provide us with significant historic detail spanning some thirty years, it is more than just another history book. Tucked away in Joshua's pages, we find numerous examples of God's grace. Through His shepherding, God fulfills His promise of land given centuries before to Abraham (Genesis 12:6–7). Christological roots run deep here as well. These sink deep into the rich soil of antiquity, then bud out to point us to Jesus Christ. He is the New Testament Joshua who conquered sin, death, and the devil on our behalf, giving us an eternal kingdom (Luke 12:32).

Any outline of this book is complete only when viewed against the dynamic role of the Promised Land, for in this divine drama God alone is the keeper of every promise (Joshua 21:43–45; 23:14).

I. Israel prepares to occupy the land (1:1–5:12)
   - A. The Lord strengthens Joshua (1:1–9)
   - B. Israel participates (1:10–18)
   - C. Rahab and the spies (Chapter 2)
   - D. Israel crosses the Jordan (Chapter 3)
   - E. Joshua erects two memorials (Chapter 4)
   - F. Circumcision and Passover renewed (5:1–12)

II. Canaan captured (5:13–12:24)
   - A. Jericho falls (5:13–6:27)
   - B. Achan's sin (Chapter 7)
   - C. Destruction of Ai (8:1–29)
   - D. The covenant renewed (8:30–35)
   - E. Gibeonite deception (Chapter 9)
   - F. The sun stands still (10:1–15)
   - G. Five Amorite kings (10:16–28)
   - H. Southern campaign (10:29–43)
   - I. Northern campaign (11:1–15)
   - J. Victories recapped (11:16–12:24)

III. The allotment of the land (Chapters 13–21)
   A. Land left unconquered (13:1–7)
   B. Division of land east of the Jordan (13:8–33)
   C. Division of land west of the Jordan (Chapters 14–19)
   D. Cities of refuge (Chapter 20)
   E. Levitical towns (Chapter 21)

IV. The heirs of the land respond (Chapters 22–24)
   A. Settling a misunderstanding (Chapter 22)
   B. Joshua's farewell (Chapter 23)
   C. The covenant renewal at Shechem (24:1–27)
   D. Burials in the Promised Land (24:28–33)

Introduction

The Book of Joshua draws its name from the central character of the book: Joshua, son of Nun. In the Hebrew Old Testament, this book is the first of four known as the former prophets, which include Judges, Samuel, and Kings. Although each of these books is found in the Christian canon, Joshua is also listed among the historical books, alongside Judges, Ruth, 1 Samuel, 2 Samuel, 1 Kings, 2 Kings, 1 Chronicles, 2 Chronicles, Ezra, Nehemiah, and Esther. Viewed on a timeline, these twelve books provide a history of the Jewish people over a period of approximately one thousand years.

However, by placing Joshua among the historical books of the Bible, there is a tendency to look only at its historicity. To do so means ignoring the many principal themes of this book. First, Joshua contains a bold reminder that it is the inspired and prophetic Word of God (Joshua 3:9–13). Second, Joshua delivers a message of Law and Gospel intended to bring its readers face-to-face with moral corruption and God's abundant grace (Joshua 21:43–45; 24:1–15). Third, Joshua's prophecy finds fulfillment in Jesus Christ. Christology is intricately woven into its pages, a Christology our Lord proclaims when He exalts Old Testament prophets and prophecies (Luke 24:25, 27, 44). Fourth, the Book of Joshua reveals God's faithfulness. Joshua unabashedly proclaims that God has kept His promise to Israel, the Promised Land of their inheritance (Joshua 21:43–45; 23:14).

For you and me, the Old Testament promises recounted in Joshua have New Testament significance. God grafts us into His kingdom through the saving grace of His own Son. As baptized believers in Jesus Christ, we are made "heirs of the promise" (Galatians 3:26–29; Romans 4:13–17; Hebrews 6:17; James 2:5). Jesus has become for us a new and greater Joshua by virtue of His sinless life, His suffering, His death, and His resurrection. Through Christ alone, our eternal inheritance is assured. The God of Abraham, Isaac, and Jacob affirms Himself to a man, Joshua, just as He affirms Himself to us through His precious Son, Jesus Christ. Let us now prepare to meet God in the pages of His revealed Word in Joshua and learn that with Him there are no broken promises (Joshua 21:43–45). Because geography provides such an important backdrop in the Book of Joshua, it is highly recommended that the Bible study leader provide maps for study participants, such as those appearing in *Joshua*, by Adolph L. Harstad in the Concordia Commentary Series.

Lesson 1

God Prepares Israel

Joshua is the sixth book of the Old Testament, and its placement comes on the heels of the Pentateuch or "the Five Books of Moses." There are some disagreements about Joshua's authorship, but the best explanation is that Joshua wrote it, and that the last five verses were added after his death. Consider these facts that we know: (1) The author was present when these events took place (Joshua 5:1 is written in first person), (2) He wrote before King David drove the Jebusites from Jerusalem (Joshua 15:63), (3) A portion was written after Joshua's death (Joshua 24:29–33) by an unknown author, and (4) All of Joshua is written under divine inspiration (Joshua 3:9).

The Book of Joshua takes its name from Joshua, son of Nun, the central character in this book of prophetic history. We learn about him for the first time in Exodus 17 when Moses sends troops to face the Amalekites. In battle, Joshua does as Moses ordered (Exodus 17:10). Moses changed his name from Hoshea or "salvation" to Joshua or "the Lord is salvation" (Numbers 13:16). In Greek, the word *Joshua* can also be spelled "Jesus." As you study the Book of Joshua, take time to note how the life of Joshua points to Jesus, who provides salvation for all humankind, not just the Israelites. Also, watch as God faithfully keeps His promises, including Israel's Old Testament land inheritance (Genesis 12:6–7).

Setting the Stage

Historically, we can place the conquest of Canaan in the year 1406 BC. Joshua was about eighty at the time. He was born during the Egyptian captivity, survived forty years of slavery in Egypt, and lived through the forty years of desert wandering. God used these years to refine Joshua's faith. Now, at last, Joshua is ready to take over the awesome responsibility of succeeding Moses and leading God's people into the Promised Land (Deuteronomy 31).

1. Take a moment to familiarize yourself with God's covenant to Abraham (Genesis 12:6–7; 13:14–17; 15:1–21; 17:1–8).

2. In Genesis 15:6, why does God declare Abraham righteous? (See also Hebrews 11:11.)

3. Genesis 17:18–21 names the inhabitants who will occupy Canaan when Abraham's descendants inherit it. Identify them. (We will encounter them again as we travel through the Book of Joshua.)

Preparations Made

As the Book of Joshua opens, the Israelites, all two to three million of them, are spread out on the plains of Moab east of the Jordan. They have just completed a thirty-day mourning period for Moses (Deuteronomy 34:8). Upon Moses' death, Joshua, son of Nun, succeeds him (Deuteronomy 34:9).

4. Read Joshua 1:1–4. Who comes quickly to Joshua after the mourning period is ended? What is his plan?

5. Joshua 1:5–9 provides some powerful words of encouragement for Joshua. List the encouraging words God speaks, noting what God teaches about His Law.

6. After reading Joshua 1:10–18, discuss Joshua's first course of action. The Rubenites, Gadites, and the half tribe of Manasseh were given territory east of the Jordan River but pledged their military support later (Numbers 32). What does Joshua ask of them? What is their reply? Is there any indication of the seriousness of their pledge? If so, what is it?

Joshua 2 contains a familiar story. Refresh your memory by reading this account. In 1406 BC, Jericho was a walled city with diplomatic ties to Egypt. Like many other Canaanite cities of its day, Jericho was ruled by a local king. Citizens lived outside the city walls, seeking shelter inside the city during attacks.

7. Before undertaking the first campaign of the Canaanite wars, what does Joshua do? To whom do these individuals go, and what is her profession?

8. Reread Joshua 2:8–13. What evidence do you find there to support the statement that Rahab already had faith in the Lord before the spies arrived?

9. As a guarantee against killing Rahab during the heat of battle, what sign must she provide for protection? God shows grace toward Rahab, and God-given faith acts in love (Galatians 5:6). How does Rahab demonstrate her faith? How might her response apply to Christians like you and me?

10. How is the reaction of the two spies alike or different from that of the twelve spies Moses sent into Canaan forty years before?

Compare and contrast Numbers 13:26–33 with Joshua 2:24. What might cause such a difference in attitude?

God's Word for Today

11. The land of Canaan provides the stage for God's divine drama. Take a moment to read Genesis 12:1–3 and the sevenfold promise God made Abraham. Especially note the words "and in you all the families of the earth shall be blessed." (For help interpreting this blessing, consult John 1:29.)

12. God's Word touched Rahab's heart. In response, she shed her old Canaanite religion. Read Matthew 1:1–16. How did God use the faith of this former Canaanite prostitute? What message does this offer you and me as we daily struggle against our sinful flesh?

In Closing

Encourage participants to begin the following activities:

- Consult a Bible dictionary for additional information on the Jordan River.
- Consider how Psalm 51:14 applies to Rahab.
- Read Joshua 3:1–5:12 to prepare for the next session.

Close by singing or reading in unison the words of "Chief of Sinners Though I Be" (*LW* 285). As you do, especially note stanza 2 and its reference to God seeking us out in our sin, just as He did Rahab and just as He does you and me.

Chief of sinners though I be,
Jesus shed His blood for me,
Died that I might live on high,

Lives that I might never die.
As the branch is to the vine,
I am His, and He is mine.

Oh, the height of Jesus' love,
Higher than the heav'ns above,
Deeper than the depths of sea,
Lasting as eternity!
Love that formed me—wondrous thought—
Found me when I sought Him not.

Only Jesus can impart,
Balm to heal the wounded heart,
Peace that flows from sin forgiv'n,
Joy that lifts the soul to heav'n,
Faith and hope to walk with God
In the way that Enoch trod.

Chief of sinners though I be,
Christ is all in all to me;
All my wants to Him are known,
All my sorrows are His own.
He sustains the hidden life
Safe with Him from earthly strife.

O my Savior, help afford
By Your Spirit and Your Word!
When my wayward heart would stray,
Keep me in the narrow way;
Grace in time of need supply
While I live and when I die.

Lesson 2

Crossing the Jordan

The spies have returned. Their favorable report that "the LORD has given all the land into our hands. And also, all the inhabitants of the land melt away because of us" (Joshua 2:24) echoed through the Israelite camp on the plains of Moab. The Lord is poised to fulfill His promise of land for His people (Genesis 12:7). Looking westward from the encampment, one can imagine the joy of seeing a land promised hundreds of years before. Now it appears only one obstacle stands in the way before the clamor of war can begin: the Jordan River.

As the Israelites wait, it is important to learn more about the Jordan. We can trace its source to the snowy peaks of Mount Hermon. (Take time to locate Mount Hermon on a map of the Holy Land.) In the spring, melting snow fills the Sea of Galilee and pours out into the Jordan. From there it makes its way south to the Dead Sea, a distance of about 70 miles as the crow flies, twisting and turning the whole way, making a 70-mile trip into a 200-mile trek. On its journey, the Jordan drops nearly 2,600 feet before it empties into the Dead Sea, which is itself some 1,300 feet below sea level. Because of this marked descent, the Jordan River is often called "the Descender."

The public ministry of Jesus begins in the Jordan River with His Baptism (Matthew 3:13–17), when He heard the words of His Father, "This is My beloved Son, with whom I am well pleased" (Matthew 3:17). Jesus, too, crossed the Jordan River just as the Israelites did centuries before. Within three years, He would go the way of the cross, taking the sins of the whole world on Himself and securing eternal life for all those who believe in Him.

Facing Your Fears

Thickets of brush and other semitropical trees line the Jordan's banks. Wild animals, including lions, make their home there. In 1406

BC, the Jordan was wider than it is now. In some cases, it was 90 to 100 feet across, with depths of 12 feet. A zigzag current made crossing difficult at best. Worst of all, when the Israelites wanted to cross it, it was Abib, the first month of a new Hebrew year, when harvest begins and the snow melts on Mount Hermon. At this time of year, the Jordan would overflow her banks (Joshua 3:15). Under normal conditions, this would not be a good time to cross the Jordan, but it's the Lord's time.

13. Take a few minutes to discuss any other information you learned about the Jordan River after consulting your Bible dictionary or map.

14. How might you react if you came face-to-face with the Jordan River of 1406 BC?

15. Describe a time when you faced a seemingly insurmountable situation.

16. How might knowing that God is gracious and always with you calm your fears?

A Dramatic Crossing

17. Read Joshua 3:1–17. After moving from the plains of Moab to an area near the Jordan River, the Israelites prepared to cross. What was the signal to move out? What was so reassuring about this signal?

18. Joshua commanded the Israelites to consecrate themselves in preparation for what God would do. According to Exodus 19:10, what did that mean?

19. What happened when the feet of priests carrying the ark of the covenant touched the Jordan River? Does this type of river crossing sound familiar? If so, where have you heard something like this before?

20. Read Joshua 4:1–24. How many stone memorials were erected after the Israelites crossed the Jordan? Where were they? How many stones were there in each memorial, and what is the significance behind this number? What was the purpose for which these memorials were constructed?

21. Joshua 4:19 provides the date of the Jordan crossing. What is significant about that date in Jewish history (Exodus 12:2–3)?

22. A twofold reason for the Lord's dramatic river crossing is revealed in Joshua 4:23–24. Explain those two reasons that along with Joshua 4:4, 7 present an early catechism for the Hebrew children.

23. Read Joshua 5:1–12. How did the Amorite and Canaanite kings react to Israel's crossing the Jordan? God commands the reinstatement of a covenant sign, which marks men with a pledge of

God's commitment to them. What is it? How does this sign confirm God's promise to Abraham (Genesis 17:10–11)?

God's Word for Today

24. The Old Testament rites of circumcision and Passover gave way to the New Testament rites. What are those rites according to Colossians 2:11–13 and Matthew 26:26–29?

25. Explain the power and significance of Baptism (Romans 6:3–10) and the power and significance of Holy Communion (Matthew 26:26–28; Hebrews 9:13–14).

26. How might the words of Joshua 5:4–7 and Galatians 3:10–13 demonstrate a message of Law and Gospel?

In Closing

Encourage participants to begin the following activities:

- Discuss the message sent by God when He assigns the ark of the covenant to lead the procession into the Jordan River.
- Think about how the campsite near Jericho ties into Psalm 23:5.
- Consult your Bible dictionary for information on the city of Jericho.
- Read Joshua 5:13–7:26 to prepare for the next session.

Close by singing or reciting in unison the words of "Thy Strong Word" (*LW* 328:1–2, 6).

Thy strong word did cleave the darkness;
At Thy speaking it was done.
For created light we thank Thee,
While Thine ordered seasons run.
Alleluia, alleluia!
Praise to Thee who light doth send!
Alleluia, alleluia!
Alleluia without end!

Lo, on those who dwelt in darkness,
Dark as night and deep as death,
Broke the light of Thy salvation,
Breathed Thine own life-giving breath.
Alleluia, alleluia!
Praise to Thee who light doth send!
Alleluia, alleluia!
Alleluia without end!

God the Father, light-creator,
To Thee laud and honor be.
To Thee, Light of Light begotten,
Praise be sung eternally.
Holy Spirit, light-revealer,
Glory, glory be to Thee.
Mortals, angels, now and ever
Praise the holy Trinity!

Pray together: Lord, we praise You for Your faithfulness. You brought Your covenant people through the Red Sea and kept them in Your care for the forty years of wilderness wandering. You safely led them through the Jordan River, pledging to help drive out the Canaanites and fulfilling Your promise of land given to Abraham. Through Your faithfulness, Your Son, the Savior of all humankind, would be born in this land. For Your faithfulness, we thank You. Amen.

Lesson 3

Jericho: The Conquest Begins

At the time of the Israelite conquest, Jericho was perhaps the oldest city on earth. Archeologists believe the city took its name from its worship of the moon, hence the name Jericho or "Moon City." The religious practices of this city most likely included both male and female prostitution, incest, homosexuality, and even the sacrifice of children, expressly forbidden as hideous in the eyes of the Lord (Leviticus 18; 20). Among the foundations of homes and temples, researchers have unearthed funerary jars containing the remains of small children often sacrificed to the pagan god Molech. It is easy to draw a comparison between Jericho at the time of Joshua and Sodom at the time of Abraham. Each city seemed ripe for the righteous judgment of God.

The old city of Jericho has long been associated with Tel es-Sultan, located about a mile west of the modern city of Jericho. Its setting in 1406 BC was along the major trade routes that struck into the heart of Canaan. In addition, it was close enough to the Jordan to control the fresh spring water supply for the area. Jericho was essentially an oasis city encompassing some 9 to 12 acres behind a fortified wall. Within the ruins at Tel es-Sultan are ancient granaries still filled with grain. If this location is the Jericho of Joshua's time, such a discovery is in harmony with the biblical accounts of the conquest. Indeed, Jericho fell quickly during the month of harvest (Abib) when recent crops filled the granaries. One would typically expect to find empty granaries from the customary depletion of crops associated with typical siege warfare, but such is not the case at Tel es-Sultan.

God's judgment is at hand. We are about to see Law and Gospel played out in a drama involving Jericho and later the conquest of Ai. God's anger burns against each city. Between each episode is the story of a man who brings shame on the nation of Israel, yet God's grace provides a wonderful example for those who trust in Him.

27. Discuss information on Jericho you found by consulting a Bible dictionary.

28. What safety measures might we have found in Jericho had we visited in 1406 BC?

God Prepares Joshua

29. Beginning with Joshua 5:13 and continuing through 12:24, we are entering a new phase in our study of the Book of Joshua. We witness the Lord delivering in full the land inheritance promised to His Old Testament people. Before the conquest begins, perhaps when Joshua was inspecting Jericho's fortifications from afar, an incident of lasting impact occurs. Read and discuss this account in Joshua 5:13–15.

30. This incident is similar to that of Moses and the burning bush (Exodus 3:1–6). Explain.

Jericho Falls

31. Read Joshua 6:1–27. This chapter is perhaps the best-known chapter in our study. Explain the Lord's strategy for conquest.

32. In the Bible, the number 7 is the number of completeness. How many references to that number are found in verses 1–5? What might the use of 7 mean here?

33. God's judgment against Jericho is Law. What instance shows God's grace (Gospel) in Joshua 6:1–27? Where was Rahab placed after her rescue? Where did she reside later? Explain what such a move means (Hebrews 11:31; Matthew 22:32).

34. When it was captured, the city of Jericho and everything in it, except Rahab and her family, was dedicated to the Lord. This practice was known as *cherem*. What did this mean to the inhabitants of Jericho (Joshua 6:24)?

35. Discuss the curse Joshua levels against Jericho (Joshua 6:26). Why might God issue such a curse? Now look at what happened to the wicked Ahab when he attempted to rebuild the city (1 Kings 16:34).

Achan's Sin

Begin this section by reading Joshua 7:1–26.

36. What was Achan's sin, and what did it mean to the entire Israelite community? How did Joshua become aware of this sin, and what did he do about it?

37. For twenty-first-century Christians, Achan's punishment seems cruel and harsh. However, what is the punishment for sin as God prescribes through St. Paul (Romans 6:23a)? A third stone memorial is erected above Achan's remains (Joshua 7:26). How might this stone memorial serve as a reminder of the destructive nature of sin?

God's Word for Today

38. Jewish tradition holds that Jeremiah, one of Israel's great prophets, was a descendant of Rahab. Jeremiah wrote, "The days are coming, declares the LORD, when I will raise up for David a righteous Branch" (Jeremiah 23:5). Of whom does Jeremiah speak? What will the coming "righteous Branch" mean to you and me (Romans 6:23b)?

39. Apply Ephesians 2:4–5 to the life of Rahab and to your own life.

In Closing

Encourage participants to begin the following activities:

- Discuss what God desired from Achan when he was accused of stealing the *cherem*.
- Discuss other cases where the Law prescribed the death penalty (see Deuteronomy 13:7–11; Leviticus 24:16; 20:2, 27; Numbers 15:32–36).
- Consult a Bible dictionary or other reliable source for information on the peoples living in Canaan at the time of the Israelite conquest.
- Read Joshua 8:1–9:27 to prepare for the next session.

Close by singing or reading together the words of “A Mighty Fortress Is Our God” (*LW* 298:1–2). Note how stanza 2 relates to Joshua’s encounter with the commander of the Lord’s army.

A mighty fortress is our God,
A trusty shield and weapon;
He helps us free from ev’ry need
That hath us now o’ertaken.
The old evil foe
Now means deadly woe;
Deep guile and great might
Are his dread arms in fight;
On earth is not his equal.

With might of ours can naught be done,
Soon were our loss effected;
But for us fights the valiant One,
Whom God Himself elected.
Ask ye, Who is this?
Jesus Christ it is,
Of sabaoth [hosts] Lord,
And there’s none other God;
He holds the field forever.

Pray: Lord of hosts, You came to the aid of Your people Israel. Now, through Your only Son, Jesus Christ, You strengthen and protect both Jew and Gentile alike who believe in Him. Send Your Holy Spirit, we pray, to guide our lives. Make us living memorials to Your righteousness. Speak to us through Your Holy Word, and then embolden us through the Lord’s Supper. Keep us daily mindful of our Baptism. We pray in Jesus’ name. Amen.

Lesson 4

Central Campaign: Part I

Jericho is destroyed. Ai has survived Joshua's original onslaught because of the sin of Achan. Now, the Lord has avenged Himself on Achan for stealing property the Lord had claimed for Himself. A third stone monument marks the spot of Achan's burial. Before we return to our biblical narrative, we will spend a few moments uncovering the identity of those nations living in Canaan at the time of Israel's conquest. These nations are identified as the Canaanites, Hittites, Hivites, Perizzites, Girgashites, Amorites, and Jebusites (Joshua 3:10). Seven nations occupy Canaan; seven nations face God's wrath.

The commonality of these nations stem from their relationship to Noah (Genesis 10:1–19). Only the Perizzites escape mention here. Every other nation finds origins in Canaan, the son of Ham, the son of Noah. In Genesis 9, we learn how Noah became drunk and lay naked in his tent. Ham discovered his father and dishonored him while he was naked. When Noah recovered, Ham's dishonor was brought to his attention. As punishment, Ham's son Canaan and his descendants were cursed. Deuteronomy 18:9–11 lists the misdeeds found among the Canaanites, some of which we have examined previously: divination, sorcery, child sacrifice, witchcraft, and sexual deviance. The tribes occupying Canaan held these things in common, but where did they live?

The Canaanites lend their name to the land and a tribe within it. They settled along the Mediterranean Sea and along the Jordan River (Numbers 13:29; Joshua 5:1; 11:3). Their Semitic alphabet later developed into the Hebrew and Northwest Semitic languages and later Greek, Latin, and even the English language. The Amorites settled the south slopes of the Judean Mountains (Deuteronomy 1:7, 19–20). The Jebusites lived in the mountains, making Jerusalem their capital city (Numbers 13:29; Joshua 11:3). The Hittites settled the northeast corner of the Mediterranean after migrating from Russia, where they are related to the Mongols. The Hivites settled the area below Mount Hermon and the Lebanon Mountains and the area around Gideon (Joshua 9:7; 11:3; Judges 3:3), while the Girgashites lived west of the Jordan River (Joshua 24:11). Little is known about the Perizzites except the mention of them living in the forestland (Joshua 24:11). These are the inhabitants of the land at the time God handed it over to the Israelites under Joshua.

40. Discuss additional information about these people that you found in your Bible dictionary or other reliable sources.

41. Can you think of nations today who might resemble ancient Canaan? Would God punish them as He did Canaan at the time of Joshua?

The Destruction of Ai

42. Read Joshua 8:1–29. Once atonement for Achan's sin is complete, what reassurance of victory does God convey to Joshua?

43. Describe God's plan of attack against Ai. After victory is achieved, how are the citizens of Ai treated? How is this similar or dissimilar to the treatment of the citizens in Jericho? What of the booty?

44. The city of Bethel was near Ai. What other events in Jewish history occurred at Bethel (Genesis 12:8; 28:10–19)?

45. Ai means "the ruin." Why is this name appropriate, and where is a fourth stone monument constructed in Canaan? Explain how this monument ties in with the words of Romans 2:5.

Covenant Renewal

46. Following consecutive victories at Jericho and Ai, the Hebrew people travel to the valley between Mount Ebal and Mount Gerizim. (Locate the region on a map.) Here they worship. One would think that the Israelites might be vulnerable to attack, but the Lord protects them. Highlight the covenant renewal ceremony (Joshua 8:30–35).

47. Joshua copied the Law of Moses on stones. What is the purpose behind these stones inscribed with the Law? (You might find Deuteronomy 4:5–6 helpful as you prepare your answer.)

48. During the worship service, Joshua read the blessings and curses aloud (Deuteronomy 28). Read 28:15, 36–37. Was it possible for the Israelites to lose the Promised Land? Explain.

Deceiving Gibeonites

49. After reading Joshua 9, discuss how the Gibeonites pulled off a ruse. Discuss words in our text that indicate the Gibeonites feared

God and that this fear drove them to seek sanctuary among the Israelites.

50. When the Gibeonite deception was discovered, a theological dilemma arose. Explain. How was the matter resolved? How does the assignment given the Gibeonites fulfill Noah's curse (Genesis 9:25–27)?

God's Word for Today

51. The Gibeonites were cursed, and on the cross so was our Lord and Savior Jesus Christ. Explain what Jesus' curse means for you and me (Galatians 3:13–14). Discuss how Jesus Christ fulfills all the Lord's promises (2 Corinthians 1:17–20).

In Closing

Encourage participants to begin the following activities:

- Study how the covenant renewal ceremony completed what Moses prescribed in Deuteronomy 11:26–32.
- Discuss how the Gibeonite curse was a blessing for the Israelites.
- Read Joshua 10:1–28 to prepare for the next session.

Close by singing or saying together the words of "Lord, Keep us Steadfast in Your Word" (*LW* 334).

Lord, keep us steadfast in Your Word;
Curb those who by deceit or sword
Would wrest the kingdom from Your Son
And bring to nought all He has done.

Lord Jesus Christ, Your pow'r make known,
For You are Lord of lords alone;
Defend Your holy Church that we
May sing Your praise triumphantly.

O Comforter of priceless worth,
Send peace and unity on earth;
Support us in our final strife
And lead us out of death to life.

Pray together: Lord, thank You for sending Your Holy Spirit to guide us as we study Your Word. We ask that You increase our faith as we learn about Your faithfulness recorded in Joshua. With each printed word, may we draw ever closer to Your Son, Jesus Christ. All nations are indeed blessed through faith in Him as their Lord and Savior. Blessed Father, thank You for keeping every promise You've ever made. We pray in Jesus' name. Amen.

Lesson 5

Central Campaign: Part II

Before we return to the Bible to learn more about Israel's central Canaan campaign, a discussion about warfare might prove helpful. We may be horrified when we read in Joshua that of all the residents in Jericho only Rahab and her family were spared (6:17) or that no one survived at Ai (8:25). We might be repulsed when we read that the king of Ai was killed and his body hung from a tree until sunset (8:29). These examples appear to contradict what the apostle John teaches when he writes, "God is love" (1 John 4:8, 16). We might wonder, "How can a loving God approve of such things?"

War has it roots in Satan, not God. Satan's rebellion led to his expulsion from heaven along with his minions (Revelation 12:4). Lashing back at God, Satan lures Adam and Eve into sin (Genesis 3). In contrast, God's response is swift and loving. From this point forward, animosity will exist between Satan and man, culminating in the Lord's great victory in Christ on the cross (Genesis 3:15; Colossians 1:19–20). As Christians, we must know that war will continue to exist as long as we live in a sinful world. A second point is even more critical to our understanding. Divine warfare is God's means of salvation for His chosen people. God declares war on death until it is swept away by Christ's blood on the cross. In his commentary on Joshua, Adolph Harstad puts it this way:

> To comprehend the twofold meaning of the military conquest of Canaan by Israel in the book of Joshua, we need to bear in mind that the LORD is a God of Law and Gospel, judgment and salvation. He damns the impenitent to eternity in hell and justifies penitent believers, making them heirs of eternal life in the new heavens and new earth. (*Joshua*, Concordia Commentary [CPH, 2004], p. 259)

As Christians, when we read Joshua we must keep in mind that God overlooked sin in Canaan for a long time. Now, the Israelites, at God's directive, are destroying the Canaanites and inheriting the land sin caused them to forfeit.

52. Comment on the statement, "God declared war on the Canaanites so that Jesus, the Prince of Peace, might be born in the land promised to Abraham" (see Genesis 12:3).

53. Review your comments on how the Gibeonite curse was actually a blessing for God's people.

A Five-King Conspiracy

Read Joshua 10:1–6.

54. Identify and then locate on a map the cities involved in this conspiracy against the Israelites.

55. The head of the conspiracy was Adoni-Zedek, king of Jerusalem. This marks the first time that the name Jerusalem appears in the Bible. Who are the people of Jerusalem, and what was the city's former name (Judges 19:10–11)? What are Adoni-Zedek's reasons for war, and whom do they attack first? How do the Gibeonites respond?

56. At the time of Abraham, a different king lived in Jerusalem, then called Salem or "peace." Who was this king (Genesis 14:18–20)? According to the Book of Hebrews, Jesus is a priest after the order of

Melchizedek (Hebrews 5:6). What does this tell you about the king who once ruled Jerusalem contrasted to Adoni-Zedek who now rules?

The Lord Strikes Back

Read Joshua 10:7–15.

57. What indications do we find in our text that the battle is waged by God and that Joshua's forces are only instruments in His mighty hand?

58. The Valley of Aijalon is located west of Gibeon and some 14 miles northwest of Jerusalem. After an all-night march through steep terrain some 3,000 feet higher than their base camp at Gilgal, the Israelite forces launched a surprise attack on the Amorite forces. Their attack pushed their enemy into this valley. What happened next (Joshua 10:12–13)? How might this event bolster the Israelite forces' confidence in Joshua?

59. Through the years, some scholars have sought to explain away the events in Joshua 10:12–13. In what should Christians place their trust (2 Timothy 3:15–17)?

Finish the account of this event by reading Joshua 10:16–28.

60. Contrast the account of the five Amorites kings found in Joshua 10:1–4 with that of 10:16. What has caused such a change?

61. In ancient times, it was customary for a victorious king to place his feet on the neck of a defeated enemy (Joshua 10:24). How might this be symbolic of Christ's victory over Satan (Genesis 3:15; John 12:31–32; 1 John 3:8b)?

62. What happened to the five kings and the king of Makkedah? Where was a fifth stone memorial erected by Israel?

God's Word for Today

63. Some people believe that the God of the Old Testament is only Law-oriented. Refute this belief while examining this statement: God acts in terms of Law *and* Gospel in the Old Testament as exemplified in His dealing with the Gibeonites and the Amorites.

64. Where did God's wrath rain down on one man (Law) bringing salvation (Gospel) to you and me (Matthew 27:45–46)?

In Closing

Encourage participants to begin the following activities:

- In Joshua, we see a man unafraid to pray to God for help (Joshua 10:12–13). Discuss how this Joshua resembles Jesus, our New Testament Joshua.
- Discuss how Israel's stone memorials served as visual aids to God's Old Testament people and how Christians today use objects to remind them of God's love and grace.
- Read Joshua 10:29–12:24 to prepare for the next session.

Close by singing or reciting together the words of "We Sing the Almighty Power of God" (*LW* 441:1–2, 6). Notice how stanza 2 echoes the words of Joshua 10:13–14.

We sing th'almighty power of God,
Who bade the mountains rise,
Who spread the flowing seas abroad
And built the lofty skies.

We sing the wisdom that ordained
The sun to rule the day;
The moon shines too at His command,
And all the stars obey.

On You each moment we depend;
If You withdraw, we die.
Oh, may we never God offend,
Our God, forever nigh!

Close with the following prayer: Dear Lord, Your mighty hand protected Your people. You watched over the Gibeonites, sending the Israelites to protect them. You stopped the sun in the sky to provide illumination for Your people. You darkened the sky on the day that You turned Your wrath on Your Son for our sins. For that blessed day, we thank You. In Jesus' name we pray. Amen.

Lesson 6

Northern and Southern Campaigns

The conquest of central Canaan was complete. By God's gracious hand, Joshua subdued the five kings united under Adoni-Zedek. Only the southern and northern regions remained in a conquest that provides a quick read in our Bibles. Each narrative easily flows into another. We might conclude that the conquests related here occurred rapid fire over a period of months. Such is not the case at all. How long did this conquest take? The answer to this question is found in the Bible itself. As we look at additional campaigns, we will find the words, "Joshua made war a long time with all those kings" (Joshua 11:18). We will learn that the conquest was not completed quickly. Are there other helpful keys? In Joshua 14:7, Caleb reveals he was forty when the thirty-eight years of desert wandering began (Deuteronomy 2:14). This makes him seventy-eight when he crossed the Jordan. Caleb states his age at eighty-five (Joshua 14:10) at the conclusion of major hostilities. From these facts, we can conclude that the period of conquest was about seven years.

God gave the Canaanites adequate time to repent of their sins. Jericho had heard how God had rescued the Israelites (Joshua 2:9–11). Yet the Canaanites chose not to repent. The salvation of Israel was made known to the other Canaanite unbelievers (Joshua 9:1–3; 10:1–2). They, too, chose to rebel instead of repent. We know from Joshua's treatment of the Gibeonites that the Lord is merciful. Still the question remains: What if the Canaanites had surrendered? Would not the Israelites have found themselves surrounded by a pagan culture? Would not this culture entice them away from the God who loved them? More than lives are at stake here; souls are at stake.

65. Take time to discuss how Joshua's prayer life resembles that of Jesus, our New Testament Joshua.

66. Refresh your memory about the importance of the stone memorials Israel erects during her conquest of Canaan.

The Southern Campaign

Read Joshua 10:29–43.

67. Count the number of military engagements during this campaign. Why is that number significant? (Note: Most likely more cities were captured than are actually listed.)

68. We have heard the names of some of the cities in a previous account of the five Amorite kings. What were their names, and what happened to them during this southern swing of the Israelite army?

69. Seven hundred years after its conquest, the city of Lachish would cause trouble during the Assyrian conquest (2 Kings 18:13–17; 19:8). It was also the last city to fall during a campaign waged by Nebuchadnezzar of Babylon in 587 BC. How long did the Israelites besiege this city (Joshua 10:32)? By whose hand were the Israelites victorious?

70. In Joshua 10:40–41, the southern campaign is recapped for us. On your map, note that Kadesh Barnea is about 50 miles from Beersheba, Gaza is near the coast, the Goshen listed here is most likely the eastern Negev, and Gibeon is 8 miles northwest of Jerusalem. What evidence is there that this territory was captured during one campaign? Where do the Israelites go after this campaign?

The Northern Campaign

Read Joshua 11.

71. Who is the instigator of the northern alliance? Why does he form this alliance (Joshua 11:1)?

72. Archaeologists estimate the population of Hazor at 40,000 inhabitants. Other forces were added to their army, which the historian Josephus estimated at 30,000 infantry, 10,000 cavalry, and 20,000 chariots. What was the Lord's plan, and how long did it take to complete (Joshua 11:6)?

73. Hazor comes under the *cherem*, a decree that required the city be destroyed, as well as the warring kings and civilians. However, only the booty is taken from the other cities. Why (see Deuteronomy 6:10–11)?

74. Some forty years before, at the time of the spies, a race of people living in Canaan frightened them (Numbers 13:28, 33). What

became of these people during the northern campaign, and how do the words of Matthew 8:26 apply here?

75. A completed territorial map is presented in Joshua 12:1–6. Reacquaint yourself with this area now by consulting your map. Using Mount Seir, south of the Dead Sea, extend a line north to Mount Hermon and then west from both mountains to the Mediterranean Sea. This is the area taken during seven years of conflict under God's direction and Joshua's leadership.

76. The vanquished kings are listed for us in Joshua 12:7–24. A total of thirty-one kings in all over a seven-year conquest. Why do you suppose the chronicling is so sparse at the close of hostilities?

God's Word for Today

77. The list of those who opposed God's New Testament kingdom is every bit as long as those listed in Joshua 12. Here are some Bible verses to help you start a list of your own: Luke 1:5; Matthew 2:16; Luke 13:31–33; John 18:13; Matthew 26:3–4, 57–58; Acts 4; 24:27.

78. Apply the words of Romans 8:35–39 and Colossians 2:14–15 to each of our two lists.

79. During this study, we often heard the Word of God encouraging and strengthening Joshua. How does He strengthen and encourage us (Hebrews 10:19–23)?

In Closing

Encourage participants to begin the following activities:

- Familiarize yourself with the tribal land divisions of Israel.
- Discuss the Lord's faithfulness to Joshua during the seven years of conquest.
- Read Joshua 13:1–33 to prepare for the next session.

Close by singing or saying in unison the words of "Jesus, Lover of My Soul" (*LW* 508:1–2).

Jesus, lover of my soul,
Let me to Thy mercy fly
While the nearer waters roll,
While the tempest still is high.
Hide me, O my Savior, hide
Till the storm of life is past;
Safe into the haven guide.
Oh, receive my soul at last!

Other refuge have I none;
Hangs my helpless soul on Thee.
Leave, ah, leave me not alone,
Still support and comfort me!
All my trust on Thee is stayed,
All my help from Thee I bring;
Cover my defenseless head
With the shadow of Thy wing.

Pray: Blessed Lord, thank You for providing a wonderful example of steadfast faith in the life of Your servant Joshua. Refresh us with the rich promise of eternal life through Your Son's body and blood. In His name we pray. Amen.

Lesson 7

Allotting the Transjordan

Joshua's days of conquest are over. Seven hard fought years have ended. God grants him rest. But what does this conquered land look like? What are some of its major topographical features? On the whole, Canaan is about the same size as the state of New Hampshire. As described in our previous lesson, its area stretches from Mount Hermon in the north to the Negev in the south, from the Mediterranean Sea on the west to the border of the Arabian Desert on the east. From north to south, it was a distance of 125 miles long, and it was 95 miles wide east to west. It is a total of 10,000 square miles. The new nation is centrally located and is traversed by many major trade routes connecting Europe, Asia, and Africa. God used Israel's location to bring nonbelievers in contact with Himself. Speaking of God's decrees, Moses once said, "See, I have taught you decrees and rules as the LORD my God commanded me, so that you should do them in the land that you are entering to take possession of it. Keep them and do them, for that will be your wisdom and your understanding in the sight of the peoples, who, when they hear all these statutes, will say, 'Surely this great nation is a wise and understanding people'" (Deuteronomy 4:5–6).

Through this land, Jesus carried out His three-year ministry. He was familiar with the Jordan River; John baptized Him there. He knew well Canaan's vast wilderness; He was tempted there. He knew Jerusalem; He redeemed us outside its gates. Then, from a rock-hewn tomb, He rose Easter morning and guaranteed believers eternal life. Every word found on the pages of Joshua points forward to the time of Jesus Christ. Through Joshua, God is cleansing the land of the Canaanites, clearing a path for the birth of His own Son who came in the fullness of time (Galatians 4:4; Romans 5:6).

80. Take time now to discuss the Lord's faithfulness to Joshua during the seven years of conquest.

81. Talk about a time when you were confident that God was guiding your steps. Sometimes we are sure of God's guidance at the time, and at other times we may only realize His guidance as we look back at a past event.

Lands Remaining to Be Taken

A careful examination of Canaan's geography reveals five important regions: the plains west of the Jordan, the western highlands, the rift valley, the plateau of Transjordan, and the deserts. Consult a map of these areas, and observe each as found in *Joshua* in the Concordia Commentary Series.

The plains west of the Jordan are the coastal plains of Asher, Sharon, and Philistia, as well as the central Valley of Jezreel and Esdraelon, and the Shephelah or western foothills.

The western highlands are found in upper and lower Galilee, the Basin of Manasseh, the Carmel Range, the Dome of Ephraim, and the hill country of Judah.

The Rift Valley consists of the Huleh Basin, the Sea of Galilee, the Jordan Valley, the Dead Sea, and the Arabah south of the Dead Sea.

The Plateau of Transjordan is the area east of the Jordan that is divided by four rivers: the Yarmuk, the Jabbok, the Arnon, and the Zered. Also included are the regions of Bashan, Gilead, Ammon, Moab, and Edom.

The deserts are the eastern deserts and the Negev.

Read Joshua 13:1–7.

82. Joshua is about ninety years old when God grants him rest from military campaigning. What lands are left for later conquests? Locate them on your map.

83. God will not abandon future leaders in campaigns waged against the Canaanites. How does Joshua know? Why would God reassure Joshua?

84. The Philistines are mentioned in Joshua 13:2. Their power base was the five cities of the Pentapolis: Gaza, Ashdod, Ashkelon, Gath, and Ekron. From where did the Philistines come? (See Jeremiah 47:4 and accompanying textual note in the *Concordia Self-Study Bible.*)

85. What Hebrew patriarchs knew of the Philistines (Genesis 20:1; 21:32, 34; 26:1)? Who was the most famous Philistine (1 Samuel 17:4)? The name Palestine later came to mean the whole area of Canaan.

Transjordan Land Assignments

Read Joshua 13:8–33.

86. Why does God not provide land to the Levites (Joshua 13:14; Deuteronomy 18:1–8)?

87. On a map, locate the lands God gave the tribes of Rueben, Gad, and the half-tribe of Manasseh. Who were these men (Genesis 29:30–32; 30:11; 41:51)?

God's Word for Today

88. As Christians, we hold no land inheritance from God as did God's Old Testament people. Rather, we have been promised a new heaven and a new earth (Revelation 21:1–4). On whom should we depend for our very existence (Luke 12:22–32)?

89. Compare your life to that of the ancient Israelites. The Israelites wandered; you lived in sin. They were promised a land of their own; you are promised eternal life through faith in Jesus Christ (Matthew 25:34). They believed in the coming Messiah; you believe that this Messiah is Jesus.

In Closing

Encourage participants to begin the following activities:

- Discuss why Caleb is given first choice among all land inheritors.
- Discover the ancestry of these three tribes of Israel: Judah, Ephraim, and Manasseh.
- Read Joshua 14:1–17:18 to prepare for the next session.

Close by singing or saying together the words of "God of Our Fathers" (*LW* 501:1–3).

God of our fathers, whose almighty hand
Leads forth in beauty all the starry band

Of shining worlds in splendor through the skies:
Our grateful songs before Your throne arise.

Your love divine has led us in the past;
In this free land by You our lot is cast:
Oh, be our ruler, guardian, guide, and stay;
Your Word our law, Your paths our chosen way.

From war's alarms, from deadly pestilence
Make Your strong arm our ever sure defense.
Your true religion in our hearts increase;
Your bounteous goodness nourish us in peace.

Pray: Gracious Father, we thank You for the many blessings so freely bestowed on us. Be with us now through our daily struggles, and uphold us when we fall. Send Your Holy Spirit to guide us in all that we do. We pray all of these things in Jesus' holy name. Amen.

Lesson 8

Allotment at Gilgal

Although we do not know this for certain, Jewish tradition holds that the land was allotted by drawing lots from clay urns, one that contained the names of the tribes and another containing a description of the land boundaries. It is also possible that the allotment of land involved the mysterious Urim and Thummim. These precious stones with the names of the twelve tribes of Israel printed on them were part of the breastplate worn by the high priest (Exodus 28:30). There is scriptural support for the use of the Urim and Thummim in the decision-making process (see Numbers 27:18–21). The Bible does not tell us exactly how the lots were drawn, but we know from the oft repeated word *inheritance* that the land was given by God's own hand (Joshua 14:1). As the tribes gather at Gilgal, the land west of the Jordan (Cisjordan) is allotted to Caleb, the remainder of the tribe of Judah, and the tribes of Ephraim and Manasseh. As we shall learn in our next lesson, the allotment of the remaining seven tribes does not take place at Gilgal but at Shiloh. We will discuss possible reasons behind the move from one location to another at that time.

90. In our previous lesson, you were asked to determine why Caleb was allowed to choose the land where his tribe would settle. Discuss those reasons now.

91. Take a moment to review the lineage of the twelve tribes of Israel as found in Genesis 29:32–35; 30:4–24; 35:16–18; and 48:5–6.

Caleb's Request

92. After reading a preview of tribal allotments in Canaan in Joshua 14:1–5, discuss the allotted share given to the Levites.

93. Now finish reading the remainder of Joshua 14. Match the facts we learn about Caleb with the appropriate Bible verse.

a. Was a forty-year-old spy	___ Joshua 14:12–14
	___ Deuteronomy 1:36
b. Given land where he spied	___ Joshua 14:8
c. Was eighty-five and still fit	___ Joshua 14:13
d. Put his trust in God	___ Joshua 14:7
e. Received Joshua's blessing	___ Joshua 14:10–11

94. Why did the men of Judah appear before Joshua at the same time as Caleb (Numbers 13:6)?

Judah's Allotment

95. Review Jacob's (Israel's) blessing on his son Judah (Genesis 49:8–12). It is the longest of all of Jacob's blessings. Besides prophesying military prowess, what does Jacob prophesy (vv. 10–12)? How is this, the most important of Jacob's blessings, fulfilled in Matthew 1:1–16 (note especially v. 3)?

96. Locate Judah's territory on a map of the twelve tribes of Israel. Judah's land has cities in four areas: the Negev (Joshua 15:21–32), the western foothills (vv. 33–47), the hill country (vv. 48–60), and

the desert (vv. 61–62). Discuss the special note recorded in Joshua 15:63.

97. Joshua 15:13–19 provides us with an interlude about Caleb's conquests. Explain how Othniel became Caleb's son-in-law. The words of Joshua 15:19 are rightly translated, "She said to him, 'Give me a blessing.'" How would such a translation illustrate Achsah's (Caleb's daughter) faith in the Lord?

Ephraim and Manasseh's Allotment

98. Jacob adopted Joseph's sons Ephraim and Manasseh as his own (Genesis 48:5). Read about the land inherited by these two brothers. A general description is found in Joshua 16:1–4. After reading the remaining verse of Joshua 16, locate Ephraim's territory on your map. Of what tribe was Joshua (1 Chronicles 7:20, 27)? Note also the words of Joshua 16:10.

99. Manasseh's allotment is presented in Joshua 17. Locate this area on your map. What request do the five daughters of Zelophehad make (vv. 3–4)? How had Moses previously ruled on this matter (Numbers 27:1–11)? What do the people of Joseph request of Joshua, their fellow tribesman (Joshua 17:14)? What is Joshua's answer (vv. 17–18)? What do you discover in verse 12 of our text?

God's Word for Today

100. We find a common thread weaving through Joshua 15:63; 16:10; and 17:12. What is that common thread? What does this failure indicate (Deuteronomy 28:1–14)? What application is there for you and me today?

101. Who grants Christians complete victory (1 Corinthians 15:56–57; Romans 7:24–25)?

In Closing

Encourage participants to begin the following activities:

- Learn why Shiloh became the new headquarters for the Israelite nation.
- Identify the land given to the remaining seven tribes of Israel.
- Read Joshua 18:1–19:48 to prepare for the next session.

Speak or sing together the words of "The Man Is Ever Blessed" (*LW* 388:1–2, 5–6).

The man is ever blessed
Who shuns the sinners' ways,
Among their counsel never stands,
Nor takes the scorner's place,

But makes the Law of God
His study and delight
Amid the labors of the day
And watches of the night.

How will they bear to stand
Before the judgment seat
Where all the saints at Christ's right hand
In full assembly meet?

He know and he approves
The way the righteous go;
But sinners and their works shall meet
A dreadful overthrow.

Pray: Gracious heavenly Father, You richly provided a land inheritance for Your Old Testament people. Through their inheritance, You pointed the way to the rich eternal inheritance bought at the price of Your Son. Teach us through Your Holy Spirit to continually thank You for Your gracious inheritance through faith in Him. We ask this through Christ, our Lord. Amen.

Lesson 9

Allotment at Shiloh

In Joshua 18, the headquarters for the Israelites abruptly changes. With several of the tribes taking control of their land inheritance, a more central worship locale is needed, hence the move from Gilgal to Shiloh. Take a moment to note the location of Shiloh on a map of Israel. As you do, note how Shiloh provides a focal point. At Shiloh, the Tent of Meeting or tabernacle, the dwelling place of God, is set up as prescribed in Exodus 26–27. Inside the Tent of Meeting rests the ark of the covenant, through which God manifested His presence for the Israelites. For nearly four hundred years, they will make Shiloh the seat of their worship. There the ark will rest, with the exception of a second covenant renewal ceremony at Shechem (Joshua 24:25–27). Later, it will be captured by the Philistines (1 Samuel 4:1–11). Like the area between Mount Gerizim and Mount Ebal discussed in lesson 4, the area around Shiloh provides acoustics desirable for large gatherings.

As our lesson unfolds, Caleb has received the city of Hebron as his inheritance. Canaanite lands were distributed by lot to the tribes of Judah, Ephraim, and the second half of Manasseh. The Transjordan lands are already in the hands of the tribes of Reuben, Gad, and the half tribe of Manasseh. Seven tribes remain: the descendants of Benjamin, Simeon, Zebulun, Issachar, Asher, Naphtali, and Dan have yet to receive their land. Interestingly, the lands allotted the two remaining spies, Caleb and Joshua, provide bookends for the lands allotted the twelve tribes of Israel. While God's Old Testament people receive land, it is but a foretaste to the inheritance promised to forgiven sinners like you and me (2 Peter 3:13; Revelation 21:1–4). Ours is a down payment earned at the cost of God's Son, Jesus Christ (Ephesians 1:13–14).

102. At the conclusion of our last lesson, you were asked to learn why Shiloh became the new headquarters of the Israelite nation. What did you discover?

103. There are two steps to taking the land of Canaan. The first is conquest, and the second is occupation. Explain what those two steps mean to you.

Benjamin's Allotment

104. Read Joshua 18:1–10. Joshua's words seem to cut to the chase. The remaining seven tribes are derelict in their duty to occupy Canaan (v. 3). What is Joshua's plan for surveying the land and distributing it? Where will the distribution take place, and how will it be done?

105. Finish reading the remainder of Joshua 18. Locate the territory given to Benjamin on the map of the twelve tribes of Israel included with this study. Benjamin receives two well-known cities in his territory. Name them. Jacob blesses his son Benjamin (Genesis 49:27), calling him a "ravenous wolf" toward his enemies. This blessing is prophetic for a ravenous Benjamite king will later rule Israel. Who is he (2 Samuel 9:1–2)?

Simeon and Zebulun's Allotment

106. Read about the allotment of land to Simeon and Zebulun in Joshua 19:1–16, and then locate their inheritance on your map. Jacob blesses his sons Simeon and Levi together (Genesis 49:5–7). He prophecies their scattering. The Levites are scattered throughout Canaan as priests while Simeon's descendants receive land. Note the location of their land. Beersheba is their most important city. What event occurred there (Genesis 21:22–34)?

107. Read Jacob's blessing in Genesis 49:13. Although landlocked, the Mediterranean Sea is only 10 miles from Zebulun's border on the west and the Sea of Galilee on the east, which makes sea trade possible. Additionally, the *Via Maris*, an international trade route, passes through Zebulun. Years later, a special young boy grows up in Nazareth, a city in Zebulun. Who is he (Matthew 2:21–23)?

Issachar and Asher's Allotment

108. The distribution of God's land grant to Issachar and Asher is described in Joshua 19:17–31. Read this section of Scripture, and locate their land on your map. What blessing does Jacob give his son Issachar (Genesis 49:14–15)? In fulfillment of Jacob's blessing, Issachar's land had the *Via Maris* running through its Jezreel Valley complete with donkeys and camels toting merchandise in their saddlebags.

109. Jacob's blessing of Asher is found in Genesis 49:20. Their territory includes the luscious Gulf of Acco north of Mount Carmel. This gulf provided products for international trade. But, all is not well

in Asher. What does this tribe do that causes problems for them (Judges 1:31–32)?

Naphtali and Dan's Allotment

110. Read Joshua 19:32–51, and locate the territories occupied by Naphtali and Dan. Now read Jacob's blessing for Naphtali in Genesis 49:21. Some scholars feel that Jacob's reference to Naphtali as "a doe let loose" refers to its free spirit, because it is set so far removed from the other tribes. Jesus' ministry often took Him to a major city in Naphtali. What is its name (Matthew 4:12–16)? As with Issachar and Zebulun, the *Via Maris* ran through Naphtali.

111. What difficulty did the Danites run into (Joshua 19:47)? Where did they settle instead of the land given to them by God? How does Jacob describe this son, which perhaps prophesies their treachery toward Leshem (Genesis 49:17)?

Joshua's Allotment

112. Read about Joshua's land inheritance in Joshua 19:49–51. What land does he choose, and where is this land located? The words of Psalm 145:14–16 best portray this man of God. Explain.

God's Word for Today

113. How are Joshua's words in 18:3 a ministerial application of Law and Gospel?

114. What do Joshua's words here teach you and me as twenty-first-century Christians? (Include Philippians 1:6: "He who began a good work in you will bring it to completion at the day of Jesus Christ.")

In Closing

Encourage participants to begin the following activities:

- Discuss the role the Levites performed in God's Old Testament Church.
- In a Bible dictionary, discover what is meant by the term "city of refuge."
- Read Joshua 20:1–23:16 to prepare for the next session.

Sing or say together the words of "On Galilee's High Mountain" (*LW* 320:1, 3).

On Galilee's high mountain
Christ gave the great command
In words of strength and promise
Which all can understand:
"All pow'r to Me is given
To do what I shall choose:
There I send My children,
Their witness I will use."

His strength within my weakness
Will make me bold to say
How His redeeming power

Transforms my stubborn clay;
His touch of fire ignites me,
With courage I am sent,
My tongue-tied silence broken,
With grace made eloquent.

Pray: Lord, give us the courage to boldly witness to Your abundant salvation. Amen.

Lesson 10

Levitical Allotment

The allotting of whole territories within Canaan has ended. By God's grace, each of the twelve tribes of Israel has received its inheritance. In the Cisjordan are the tribes of Judah, Simeon, Dan, Benjamin, Ephraim, a half tribe of Manasseh, Zebulun, Issachar, Asher, and Naphtali. While in the Transjordan, we find the allotted territories of Reuben, Gad, and a half tribe of Manasseh. This is the Promised Land. Now it is in the possession of the Israelites. Only two things remain: the establishment of cities of refuge, and the allotting of Levitical cities.

God established provisions for the cities of refuge before Moses died (Numbers 35:6–34; Deuteronomy 4:41–43; 19:1–5). Moses had already established three such cities east of the Jordan to protect someone guilty of an accidental death (Deuteronomy 19:8–9). At God's command, three more such cities are established west of the Jordan. As we will learn in this lesson, there were stipulations on how someone was admitted into a city of refuge and how long they were required to stay.

As for the second theme of providing Levitical cities, you may recall several instances where God affirmed that the Levites would not receive a territorial land grant as the other offspring of Jacob did (Joshua 13:14, 33; 14:3; 18:7). Instead, their land inheritance will consist of forty-eight cities with surrounding pastureland scattered throughout Canaan. Watch carefully as God strategically places these cities so that each Israelite is not too far away from a Levitical city. It is God's plan to make the Levites available to teach His Word. One Levitical duty is that they must instruct their fellow Israelites on the true teaching of what it means to have a covenant relationship with God. God's people would be strengthened by hearing about His gracious promises to them over and over.

115. Take time now to discuss the role of the Levites in Old Testament times.

116. Define what the phrase "city of refuge" means as found in a Bible dictionary or other reliable source.

Cities of Refuge

117. Read Joshua 20:1–9 and Numbers 35:16–21. What is the duty of the "avenger of blood"? The avenger of blood takes his authority from a command God gave Noah after the flood (Genesis 9:6). Explain. What does this verse teach us about capital punishment?

118. Who can flee to the safety of a city of refuge of which Moses provides further examples in Numbers 35:22–23 and Deuteronomy 19:5?

119. Talk about the process of being admitted into a city of refuge and the twofold process that must be completed before an individual can leave again. Locate each city of refuge on your map. Why might God have placed each city where He did?

120. You may recall King David committed premeditated murder in the case of Uriah the Hittite. Why was he not put to death (read

Psalm 51 as well as 2 Samuel 12:13)? What does God desire of all sinners as demonstrated through the life of David?

Levitical Cities

121. Chapter 21 marks the final phase of the allotment of Canaan. Begin this section of our study by reading Joshua 21:1–41. Where does the allotment of Levitical cities occur?

122. The Kohathites mentioned in Joshua 21:4 refer to the male heirs of Levi through his son Kohath (Exodus 6:16). In turn, Kohath had four sons, including Amram who was the father of Moses and Aaron (Exodus 16:18, 20). God appointed Aaron and his sons to be priests (Exodus 28–29). It is Levi's descendants through Kohath, through Aaron who functioned as priests who are offering sacrifices before the Lord. The other Levites served in the capacity as teachers of the Word and performed housekeeping functions in the Tent of Meeting. Locate as many cities given to the Kohathites as possible on your map. During the time of David, the Tent of Meeting will move to a more permanent home in Jerusalem. How does the location of the Kohathite cities show God's hand in the drawing of lots?

123. How is the scattering of Levitical cities throughout the twelve tribes a fulfillment of Genesis 49:5–7? Why might God scatter the Levites by placing their cities in the territory of each of the twelve tribes?

124. Joshua 21 wraps up on a very poignant note (Joshua 21:43–45). What is the purpose of these words? Why are they so very important for the Israelites to remember? How are these words similar to what the apostle John wrote in John 20:31? Review the promises God had kept, beginning with Genesis 12:2–3 and 13:14–17.

Gods Word for Today

125. Comment on this statement: "Levi's curse (Law) becomes a blessing for all of Israel (Gospel)."

126. As sinners, we deserve death (Romans 6:23a [Law]). To whom do we run as our personal city of refuge (2 Samuel 22:2–3, 33; *LW*, pp. 136–37 [Gospel])? (You might include in your discussion Romans 8:31–39 and Galatians 3:26–29.)

In Closing

Encourage participants to begin the following activities:

- Discuss the faithfulness of God compared to the fickleness of man.
- Why is it important for Christians today to teach their children about God's faithfulness?
- God gave Israel the land as He promised, yet the Northern Kingdom of Israel was taken into captivity in 722 BC and the Southern Kingdom of Judah followed in 587 BC. Why? Review Deuteronomy 28:15, 36–37.
- Read Joshua 22:1–24:33 to prepare for the next session.

Say or sing together the words of "Abide with Us, Our Savior" (*LW* 287:1–3, 5).

Abide with us, our Savior,
Nor let Your mercy cease;
From Satan's might defend us,
And give our hearts Your peace.

Abide with us, our Helper,
Sustain us by Your Word;
Let us and all Your people
To living faith be stirred.

Abide with us, Redeemer,
O Light, eternal Light;
Your truth direct and guide us
To flee from error's night.

Abide as our protector
Among us, Lord, our strength;
Let world and wily Satan
Be overcome at length.

Close with this prayer: Father in heaven, we thank You for keeping all of Your promises. We stumble and fall in our sinfulness, yet You keep Your promise to forgive us through the blood of Your Son. Make us ever mindful of Your many gifts that are richly bestowed on us as undeserving as we are. Send Your Holy Spirit, we pray, to conform our lives to Your image. Hear our prayer for Jesus' sake. Amen.

Lesson 11

God's Heirs Respond

The word *covenant* presents us with one of many recurring themes in Joshua. Soon this theme will repeat as God's covenant is renewed at Shechem in an elaborate ceremony involving all of Israel (Joshua 24). Biblical scholars teach us that Old Testament covenants were instituted by God and usually involved the shedding of blood. Recall the Lord's covenant with Noah. Deboarding the ark and moved by the Holy Spirit in a spirit of thankfulness to God, Noah built an altar and sacrificed a burnt offering (Genesis 8:20). This burnt offering involved the shedding of animal blood as part of the covenant God makes with all mankind never again to flood the land (Genesis 8:21). Why blood? The Book of Hebrews explains: "Without the shedding of blood there is no forgiveness" (9:22). Each sacrifice and covenant dramatically points forward to the one and final atoning blood sacrifice of God's own Son (Hebrews 9:11–14).

As early as the Noahic covenant is in salvation history, it is not the first shedding of blood; that distinction belongs to the time of Adam and Eve after the Fall. Here we find the first Messianic promise (Genesis 3:15) sealed in the blood of animals that God used to clothe our earliest ancestors (Genesis 3:21).

At the time of Joshua, two covenants are in play. The first is the Abrahamic with its sevenfold blessings (Genesis 12:1–3) and the promise of land (Genesis 12:7; 15:8–21). The Abrahamic covenant was one of pure grace (i.e., unconditional and irrevocable), and its Messianic promise was revealed in the words "and in you all the families on earth shall be blessed" (Genesis 12:3). The Mosiac covenant, the second covenant, taught the Israelites that keeping their inherited land was conditional (Exodus 19:5). When our study reaches chapters 23–24, be sure to note Joshua's continual pleading for the Israelites to remain faithful to God by recounting God's faithfulness to them.

Transjordan Troops Released

127. Early in our study, we watched as Joshua reminded the Gadites, Reubenites, and the half tribe of Manasseh of the vow they made to Moses (Joshua 1:12–18). Now during a speech often called Joshua's first farewell address, he addresses these troops again. What do we learn about these forces (Joshua 22:1–9)? Did these troops return to their families empty-handed? Where does this dismissal occur?

128. As a servant of God, Joshua sends these troops home with an important exhortation (Joshua 23:5). Explain.

129. After reading the remainder of chapter 22, explain the incident that stirs the blood of the Cisjordan Israelites. Who is sent to resolve this conflict? Who heads up this group? Explain how the conflict is resolved. How is the example of resolving hostilities within the Church an excellent example to follow? Discuss how this conflict resolution is or is not in harmony with the Word of Christ (Matthew 18:15–17).

Joshua's Second Farewell

130. Joshua's second farewell is recorded in chapter 23. Read this aloud. To whom is it addressed? Why is it especially important that these men hear Joshua's words as Joshua's life comes to a close?

131. List the verses in our text that recount God's faithfulness to His people.

132. Name the four practices the Israelites were to avoid, the commandment these practices violate, and the consequences for violating God's covenant.

133. Does God's faithfulness manifest itself in Joshua's warnings against apostasy and similar warnings found in Leviticus 26:14–33; Deuteronomy 28:15–68; and 29:17–27? Why or why not?

Covenant Renewal and a Third Farewell

134. Before his death, Joshua again assembled the Israelites at Shechem to renew their covenant with God. By using the phrase "presented themselves before God," Joshua is instructing future readers that the Tent of Meeting and the ark of the covenant were assembled at Shechem for this solemn service. Read the details in Joshua 24:1–27. Joshua speaks on behalf of the Lord, recounting all He has done for His people. Recount God's faithfulness found here.

135. What warnings did God give through Joshua? In this regard, how was Joshua like Moses (Deuteronomy 28–29)?

136. What pledge do the Israelites make before God and each other that day? What memorial to this pledge is erected at Shechem?

137. Our study concludes with the reading of Joshua 24:28–33. What three burials occur in these verses? What term is given to Joshua that was previously given to Moses (Joshua 1:1–2)? What does this term tell us about Joshua? Describe what is interesting about the second burial and this individual's trust in God and God's faithfulness to him (Genesis 50:25–26; Exodus 13:19)?

God's Word for Today

138. These three men, buried at the close of this divinely written book, held a common belief with Abraham and the whole community of faith—including you and me. What is that belief? Find your answer in the words of Romans 4:20–24.

In his commentary on Joshua, Adolph L. Harstad writes, "The book of Joshua has testified through its earthly and factual history that the LORD gives what he says. He wrote his fulfillment in the literal earth when he gave through Joshua the land long ago promised to Abraham. But he wrote it in a higher way when he sank a cross into the soil of that land and raised upon it his Son, the Christ, to reconcile the world to himself" (*Joshua*, Concordia Commentary [CPH, 2004], p. 826). Amen.

In Closing

Sing or speak together the words of "Rise! To Arms! With Prayer Employ You" (*LW* 303:1–2).

Rise! To Arms! With prayer employ you,
O Christians, lest the foe destroy you;
For Satan has designed your fall.
Wield God's Word, the weapon glorious;
Against all foes be thus victorious.
God will set you above them all.
Fear not the hordes of hell,
Here is Emmanuel.
Hail the Savior!
The strong foes yield
To Christ, our shield,
And we, the victors, hold the field.

Cast afar this world's vain pleasure
And boldly strive for heav'nly treasure.
Be steadfast in the Savior's might.
Trust the Lord, who stands beside you,
For Jesus from all harm will hide you.
By faith you conquer in the fight.
Take courage, weary soul!
Look forward to the goal!
Joy awaits you.
The race will run,
Your long war won,
To that great glory which we sing.

Pray: Lord, You alone are faithful. We thank You for Your servant Joshua. In Jesus' name. Amen.

Leader Notes

These notes are provided as a safety net, a place to turn for help in answering questions and for enriching discussion. It will not answer every question raised in your class. Please read it along with the questions before class. Consult it in class only after exploring the Bible references and discussing what they teach. Please note the different abilities of your class members. Some will easily find the Bible passages listed in this study; others will struggle. To make participation easier, team up members of the class. For example, if a question requires people to look up several passages, assign one passage to one group, the second to another, and so on. Divide the work. Let participants present the answers they discover.

Preparing to Teach Joshua

To prepare to lead this study, read through the Book of Joshua. You might read the introduction to Joshua in the *Concordia Self-Study Bible* or a Bible handbook. Several maps of the ancient Near East at about 1400 BC would also be of great help.

If you have the opportunity, you will find it helpful to make use of other biblical reference works in the course of your study. These commentaries can be very helpful: Adolph L. Harstad, *Joshua*, Concordia Commentary (St. Louis: Concordia Publishing House, 2004); M. H. Wondstra, *The Book of Joshua*, The New International Commentary on the Old Testament (Grand Rapids: Eerdmans, 1981); *Joshua*, People's Bible Commentary (Milwaukee: Northwestern Publishing House, 1991; reprinted by Concordia Publishing House, 2005 [revised edition]). Although it is not strictly a commentary, the section on Joshua in *The Word Becoming Flesh* by Horace Hummel (St. Louis: Concordia Publishing House, 1970) also contains valuable material for the proper interpretation of this biblical book.

Group Bible Study

Group Bible study means mutual learning from one another under the guidance of a leader. The Bible is an inexhaustible resource. No one person can discover all it has to offer. The leader should resist the temptation to give the answers and so act as an authority. This teaching approach stifles participation by individual members and can actually hamper learning. As a general rule, don't give interpretation, but try to develop interpreters. In other words, don't explain what the learners can discover by themselves. This is not to say that the leader shouldn't share insights and information gained by his or her class members during the lesson, engage them in meaningful sharing and discussion, or lead them to a summary of the lesson at the close.

Have a chalkboard and chalk or newsprint and marker available to emphasize significant points of the lesson. Rephrase your inquiries or the inquiries of participants as questions, problems, or issues. This provokes thought. Keep discussion to the point. List the answers given on the chalkboard or newsprint. Then, determine the most vital points made in the discussion. Ask additional questions to fill gaps.

The aim of every Bible study is to help people grow spiritually, not merely in biblical and theological knowledge but in Christian thinking and living. This means growth in Christian attitudes, insights, and skills. The focus of this course must be the Christ and the world of our day. The guiding question will be this: What does the Lord teach us about Himself and our life today through Joshua?

Teaching the Old Testament

Teaching the Old Testament can degenerate into mere moralizing in which do-goodism becomes a substitute for the Gospel and sanctification gets confused with justification. Actually, the justified sinner is not moved by Law but by God's grace in Christ to a totally new life. His or her faith in Christ is always at work in every context of life. Meaningful personal Christianity consists of faith flowing from God's grace in Christ and is evidenced in love for other people. Having experienced God's free grace and forgiveness through the merits of Jesus, the Christian daily works in his or her world to reflect the will of God for humanity in every area of human endeavor.

Christian leaders are Gospel-oriented, not Law-oriented. They distinguish between the two. Both Law and Gospel are necessary. The Gospel will mean nothing unless we first have been crushed by the Law and see our sinfulness. There is no genuine Christianity where faith is not followed by lives pleasing to God. In fact, genuine faith is inseparable from life. The Gospel alone gives us the new heart that causes us to love God and our neighbor.

When Christians teach the Old Testament, they do not teach it as Law but instead as books containing both Law and Gospel. They see the God of the Old Testament as a God of grace who out of love establishes a covenant of love with His people (Deuteronomy 7:6–9) and forgives their sins. Christians interpret the Old Testament using the New Testament message of fulfilled prophecy through Jesus Christ. They teach as leaders who personally know the Lord Jesus as Savior, the victorious Christ who gives all believers a new life (2 Corinthians 5:17) and a new mission (John 20:21).

Pace Your Teaching

The lessons in this course of study are designed for a study session of at least an hour in length. If it is the desire and intent of the class to complete an entire lesson each session, it will be necessary for you to summarize the content of certain answers or biblical references in order to preserve time. Asking various class members to look up different Bible passages and to read them aloud to the rest of the class will save time over having every class member look up each reference.

Also, you may not want to cover every question in each lesson. This may lead to undue haste and frustration. Be selective. Pace your teaching. Spend no more than five to ten minutes opening the lesson. During the lesson, get the sweep of meaning. Stop occasionally to help the class gain understanding of a word or concept. Allow approximately five minutes for closing the lesson and announcements.

Should your group have more than a one-hour class period, you can take it more leisurely. But do not allow any lesson to drag and become tiresome. Keep it moving. Keep it alive. Keep it meaningful. Eliminate some questions, and restrict yourself to those questions most meaningful to the members of the class. If most members study the text at home, they can report their findings, and the time gained can be applied to relating the lesson to life.

Good Preparation

Good preparation by you, the leader, usually affects the pleasure and satisfaction the class will experience.

Suggestions to the Leader for Using the Study Guide

The Lesson Pattern

This set of lessons is designed to aid Bible study, that is, to aid a consideration of the written Word of God, with discussion and personal application growing out of the text at hand.

The typical lesson is divided into these sections:

1. Theme Verse
2. Objectives
3. Questions and Answers
4. Closing

The theme verse and objectives give you assistance in arousing the interest of the group in the concepts of the lesson. Here is where you stimulate minds of the class members. Do not linger too long over the introductory remarks.

The questions and answers provide the real spadework necessary for Bible study. Here the class digs, uncovers, and discovers; it gets the facts and observes them. Your comments are needed only to the extent that they help the group understand the text. The questions in this guide, corresponding to sections within the text, are intended to help the participants discover the meaning of the text.

Having determined what the text says, the class is ready to apply the message. Having heard, read, marked, and learned the Word of God, proceed to digest it inwardly through discussion, evaluation, and application. This is done, as this guide suggests, by taking the truths found in Scripture and applying them to the world and Christianity in general and then to personal Christian life. Class time may not permit discussion of all questions and topics. In preparation, you may need to select one or two and focus on them. Close the session by reviewing one important truth from the lesson.

Remember, the Word of God is sacred, but this study guide is not. The notes in this section offer only guidelines and suggestions. Do not hesitate to alter the guidelines or substitute others to meet your needs and the needs of the participants. Adapt your teaching plan to your class and your class period. Good teaching directs the learner to discover for himself or herself. For you, the teacher, this means directing the learner, not giving the learner answers. Choose the verses that should be looked up in Scripture. What discussion questions will you ask and at what points? Write them in the margin of your Study Guide. Involve class members, but give them clear directions. What practical actions might you propose for the week following the lesson? Which of the items do you consider most important for your class?

Consider how you can best use your teaching period. Do you have forty-five minutes? an hour? or an hour and a half? If time is short, what should you cut? Learn to become a wise steward of class time.

Plan a brief opening devotion using members of the class. And be sure to take time to summarize the lesson, or have a class member do it.

Remember to pray frequently for yourself and your class. May God the Holy Spirit bless your study and your leading of others into the comforting truths of God's Christ-centered Word.

Lesson 1

God Prepares Israel

Theme verse: *Every place that the sole of your foot will tread upon I have given to you, just as I promised to Moses.*

Joshua 1:3

Objectives

By the power of the Holy Spirit working through God's Word, we will

- Learn of God's promise to be with Joshua;
- Discover how God prepares His people to receive their land inheritance;
- Journey with the spies as they reconnoiter Jericho;
- Witness the faith God worked in Rahab.

Setting the Stage

1. Review the Abrahamic covenant in Genesis 12:6–7; 13:14–17; 15:1–21; and 17:1–8. Notice that in each we see a promise of land for Abraham's descendants. Faithful to His promise, in the first few chapters of the Book of Joshua, God prepares His people to receive their land inheritance.

2. God declared Abraham righteous, and through the Holy Spirit Abraham was given the gift of faith to receive that gracious declaration. Abraham believed that God would give exactly what He promised: numerous offspring, land, and ultimately, a Savior through whom "all the families of the earth shall be blessed" (Genesis 12:3).

3. These are the people God said would be in the land at the time of the Canaanite conquest: Kenites, Kenizzites, Kadmonites, Hittites, Perizzites, Rephaites, Amorites, Canaanites, Girgashites, and Jebusites. We will encounter these people when the conquest of Canaan begins.

Preparations Made

4. Deuteronomy 34:8 reveals that the Israelites mourned the death of their great leader Moses for thirty days. At the end of this mourning period, God revealed Himself to Joshua, Moses' handpicked successor (Deuteronomy 34:9). God's plan was to give the Israelites the land He promised to Abraham many years before.

5. These are God's encouraging words to Joshua: "Be strong and courageous," and "be strong and very courageous," "Do not be frightened," and "do not be dismayed." Additionally, we find God's words of caution regarding the Law. Joshua is not to stray to the right or the left; he is to meditate on God's Law and do everything written in it. Out of love for the Lord, Joshua is to honor Him through the actions of keeping God's Law. This ability is brought about by the faith given Joshua by the Holy Spirit through God's promise.

6. Joshua's first course of action is to remind the Gadites, Reubenites, and the half tribe of Manasseh of their pledge to Moses. These two and a half tribes have already received their inherited land east of the Jordan. In return, they pledged to fight with their brothers until the land west of the Jordan is secured (Numbers 32:1–27). The Transjordan tribes of Rueben, Gad, and the half tribe of Manasseh pledge to faithfully discharge their duty as promised to Moses (Joshua 1:16–18). The seriousness of their pledge is indicated by saying they are willing to be put to death if they do not discharge it as pledged (v. 18).

7. Before undertaking his first campaign, Joshua sends two spies to reconnoiter Jericho. These men make their way to the residence of Rahab the harlot. Some scholars believe that Rahab was an innkeeper as well. What an excellent place for these two spies to learn about the city's fortifications and preparations for war.

8. The evidence of Rahab's faith before the spies arrived is seen in her words found in Joshua 2:11: "for the LORD your God, He is God in heaven above and on the earth beneath."

Such faith can only come through the working of the Holy Spirit through the Word in Rahab's life. She has heard how God has delivered His people through the Red Sea, has delivered His people through battles against the Amorites, and now sits on the other side of the Jordan ready to conquer the land God promised them. The Holy Spirit has worked faith in Rahab through this Word.

9. As a sign, Rahab must tie a scarlet cord in her window (Joshua 12:18). Rahab demonstrates her faith by protecting the spies God

brought to her home. She sends the king's men in the opposite direction than she sent Joshua's spies. God calls you and me to respect others and to guard them against all evils. If time permits, examine Luther's explanations to the Fourth through Tenth Commandments found in his Small Catechism. Review the manner in which we are to demonstrate our fear and love of God within the context of human relationships.

10. The reaction of the spies is different from that of ten of the twelve spies Moses sent into Canaan. Those ten spies fearfully reported that the Israelites could not conquer the people in the land. The remaining two, Joshua and Caleb, reported that the Israelites could conquer the land with the help of God. The difference between the spies' attitudes lies in faith that the Lord would accomplish everything He says.

God's Word for Today

11. The blessing found in God's words to Abraham is the word of the promised Savior who takes away the sin of the world (John 1:29). We know God's word to Abraham is a messianic prophecy fulfilled completely in the life, death, and resurrection of Jesus Christ.

12. Matthew 1:1–16 details the linage of Jesus. Zero in on verse 5, and you will note that Rahab's name appears in the text. God chose Rahab to be an ancestress of Christ. Although Rahab was a Gentile, God grafted her into the family tree of Jesus. Through Rahab, a sinner just like us, we see the abundance of God's grace through His Son.

Lesson 2

Crossing the Jordan

Theme verse: *As I was with Moses, so I will be with you.*

Joshua 3:7

Objectives

By the power of the Holy Spirit working through God's Word, we will

- Learn that God was with Joshua just as He was with Moses;
- Witness God's gracious presence and power in the dramatic crossing of the Jordan River;
- Watch as two memorials of God's mighty works are erected;
- Discuss the renewal of circumcision and the Passover.

Facing Your Fears

13. Take a few minutes to discuss the Jordan River. Keep in mind that at the time of its crossing, the waters raged at flood stage, which made crossing impossible without the help of God.

14. Answers will vary. Most likely conclusions will center on the fear created by having to cross such a river.

15. Answers will vary. Allow participants to discuss those times when we face insurmountable situations that are impossible to handle on our own.

16. Sometimes God places us in impossible situations to teach us to rely on Him. God knows that there are times when our faith wavers, and it is then that we should recall God's word to Joshua: "Be strong and courageous" (Joshua 1:6–7, 9). It is important to note that whenever God repeats Himself three times, He is stressing the importance of what He is teaching.

A Dramatic Crossing

17. When the ark of the covenant moves out, so do the people, a magnificent reminder that they are receiving their land inheritance by God's hand.

18. The word *consecrate* means "to set apart for God's use." Exodus 19:10 teaches that consecration often meant washing oneself as well as one's clothing, which signified an inward cleansing. This was done in preparation for witnessing God's awesome power in the Jordan crossing and conquest of Canaan.

19. When the feet of the priests carrying the ark touched the Jordan, the flow of the river immediately stopped. With clear passage, the Israelites crossed unimpeded into Canaan. The Jordan River crossing should sound familiar. It is similar to the Red Sea crossing found in Exodus 14:21–22.

20. A total of two memorials were erected, one in the middle of the Jordan and a second later that same day at the Israelite campsite at Gilgal. Twelve stones were erected for each memorial, one for each of the twelve tribes of Israel. Note that God commanded only one memorial to be placed at Gilgal. The second memorial in the Jordan was placed there at Joshua's command.

21. Joshua 4:19 dates the Jordan crossing as the tenth day of the first month, the day of the very first Passover (Exodus 12:2–3).

22. The two reasons the memorials were erected were so they might serve as a reminder of God's deliverance to future generations and also stand as a witnessing sentinel of God's mighty power to people of other nations who travel there.

23. The dramatic river crossing melted the hearts of the Amorite and Canaanite kings, signaling a time of peace for the Israelites. Such a time of peace allowed the healing of the Israelite men, all of whom are circumcised at Gilgal at the Lord's command.

God's Word for Today

24. The New Testament Sacraments replacing circumcision and Passover are Baptism (Colossians 2:11–13) and Holy Communion (Matthew 26:26–29).

25. In each Sacrament, God is at work. In our Baptism, our old, sinful self was drowned, and we were raised up again as a new creation in Christ (Romans 6:3–10). In Holy Communion, Christ gives us His

own body and blood to forgive our sins and to strengthen and preserve us in true faith to life everlasting (Hebrews 9:13–14).

26. By not keeping God's Law ("obey the voicc of the LORD" as Joshua states in 5:6), those Israelites of military age when they left Egypt died in the desert. This corresponds to Romans 6:23a. In Galatians 3:13 teaches that because of Christ we are redeemed from not keeping the Law perfectly. Christ's life and death frees us to live as a redeemed people who are no longer under the curse of the Law, which corresponds to Romans 6:23b. We thank God for His redeeming grace made possible by His own Son, who lived perfectly for us and who willingly went to the cross on our behalf.

Lesson 3

Jericho: The Conquest Begins

Theme verse: *And the LORD said to Joshua, "See, I have given Jericho into your hand, with its king and mighty men of valor."*

Joshua 6:2

Objectives

By the power of the Holy Spirit working through God's Word, we will

- Discover the Lord's plan for Jericho;
- Witness the work of the two spies sent by Joshua;
- Learn of Rahab's saving faith;
- Watch as God uses Rahab in His mighty plan of salvation.

27. Allow a few minutes of class time to discuss what was revealed about Jericho in a Bible dictionary.

28. Among Jericho's fortifications was a wall surrounding the city and a strong door designed to keep residents safe within the city. In a time of invasion, citizens would flee from the countryside and seek shelter within the fortified walls of the city.

God Prepares Joshua

29. Prior to launching his attack on Jericho, Joshua encountered a man with his sword drawn. The man identifies himself as the commander of the Lord's army; he has not come to fight for Jericho or Joshua but for the Lord. Joshua is instructed to remove his sandals, for the ground on which he walked was holy.

30. The incident recorded in Joshua 5:13–15 is similar to that of the burning bush account of Exodus in that, during a time of crisis, the Lord called Moses and strengthened him for the task ahead. As Joshua

prepared for the battle knowing the Lord was near for him just as He was for Moses, this was a great comfort. Did you also notice that in both instances the ground on which these two men of God stood was declared holy? Biblical scholars suggest that the commander of the Lord's army, who shows Himself to Joshua, was actually the pre-incarnate Jesus Christ.

Jericho Falls

31. The Lord's strategy defied the traditional siege warfare of Joshua's day. Once a day for six days, the Israelites will march silently around the city. Notice the prominent location of the ark of the covenant. This reminded the people that victory comes at God's hands and not their own. On the seventh day, the Israelites will march seven times around Jericho with the priests blowing their trumpets. At the long blast, the Israelites will shout and the city walls will tumble to the ground. All that is left is for the Israelites to enter the city to subdue it.

32. In these verses, there are three sevens. The number 7 symbolizes the complete destruction of Jericho at God's hand.

33. The rescue of the prostitute Rahab and her family must be considered pure grace. God provides her safety through the forces sent to conquer Jericho. Rahab was originally placed outside the Israelite camp, which was the traditional location for those who are not part of the Hebrew covenant community. Later, she would be brought within the covenant community and allowed to live in the camp.

34. In this case, *cherem* means that everything within the walls of Jericho would be destroyed by fire. The only exception was that the silver, the gold, and the articles of bronze and iron were to be placed into the Lord's treasury. No booty was to be taken from the city, for everything else belonged to the Lord. In later studies, we will learn that sometimes the Lord allowed the taking of booty by the conquering troops. That is not the case here.

35. Joshua's curse involved the death of the firstborn and the youngest child of anyone who rebuilt Jericho. God issued this curse through Joshua to condemn forever the apostasy of this city. Recall, if you will, the sinfulness of this community described in the introduction to this lesson. 1 Kings 16:34 teaches that King Ahab lost his firstborn and his youngest child when he rebuilt Jericho on its original spot years later.

Achan's Sin

36. Contrary to the Lord's command, Achan took *cherem* from Jericho and hid it inside his tent. Joshua 7:1 indicates that because of Achan's sin, the Lord's anger burned against all Israel. Achan's sin contaminated the whole Israelite covenant community. Joshua was told of Israel's sin as God answered Joshua's prayer of "Why?" regarding their defeat at Ai. In response, Joshua ordered the Israelites to consecrate themselves and present themselves tribe by tribe, clan by clan, and family by family until the Lord revealed Achan as the guilty party. During the presentation process, the Lord provided Achan with every opportunity to come forward and admit his guilt. However, he chose not to and suffered the consequences for his sin.

37. In Romans 6:23a, St. Paul teaches us that "the wages of sin is death." Regardless of the size of the sin, all sin merits death. The third stone memorial erected in Canaan undoubtedly afforded many opportunities for Israelite fathers to teach their children that sin brings condemnation on the entire covenant community and that sin against God merits death.

God's Word for Today

38. Jeremiah speaks of Rahab's greatest descendant, our Lord and Savior, Jesus Christ. Thanks be to God who provided His precious Son for us. Christ, our Savior, provides for us because "the free gift of God is eternal life in Christ Jesus our Lord" (Romans 6:23b).

39. Ephesians 2:4 applies both to Rahab and to us. As a prostitute, Rahab was dead in her sin, but the Holy Spirit reached into her life through the Word of God and brought her into a new life within the covenant community of God's people. Likewise, the Spirit reaches into our lives through God's Word to make us His new creation. Note the important words of Galatians 4:5; this salvation is by God's grace and not by any works we, or Rahab, have done.

Lesson 4

Central Campaign: Part I

Theme verse: *See, I [the LORD] have given into your hand the king of Ai, and his people, his city, and his land.*

Joshua 8:1

Objectives

By the power of the Holy Spirit working through God's Word, we will

- Learn of God's plan to conquer Ai;
- Witness how Joshua and his men faithfully carry out God's plan;
- Watch the covenant renewal and the deception of the Gibeonites;
- Discover how Christ's curse on the cross is our blessing.

40. Discuss information you learned about the people living in Canaan at the time of Israel's conquest.

41. At times, our own nation resembles ancient Canaan with its sanctioned killing of the unborn, moral decay promoted in the media, promotion of so-called mercy killings, and apathy toward God's Church. Yes, God will punish any society that rebels against Him. The purpose behind this punishment is to bring people to repentance and faith so they might spend an eternity with Him.

The Destruction of Ai

42. Our theme verse of Joshua 8:1 provides the reassurance that Joshua needs as he begins his campaign against Ai.

43. In an elaborate plan, several of Joshua's troops hid themselves between the cities of Bethel and Ai. Joshua feigns a frontal

attack, which the army of Ai repulses. As the Israelite army retreats, Joshua signals the ambushers to attack and destroy Ai. When Ai's army sees the smoke of their burning city, they scatter only to face destruction at the hands of the victorious Israelites. The inhabitants in Ai are all put to the sword and burned, which is similar to what happened in Jericho. The difference is that the Israelites were allowed by God to take possession of "livestock and the spoil" (Joshua 8:27).

44. In Bethel, Abraham once pitched his tent and built an altar (Genesis 12:8). It is also the site of Jacob's dream of a stairway to heaven (Genesis 28:10–19).

45. The name Ai or "the ruin" is appropriate since rubble and ruin are all that remain after the Israelites destroyed it. Joshua raised a fourth stone memorial over the city of Ai. Not only did this memorial serve as a reminder of the Israelite victory, but it also called sinful cities and nations to repentance and faith (Romans 2:5).

Covenant Renewal

46. Joshua built an altar of uncut stone on Mount Ebal, where fellowship offerings used to be sacrificed. Joshua then copied the Law of Moses on stone. With the ark of the covenant strategically placed between the people, half in front of Mount Ebal and half in front of Mount Gerizim, Joshua read aloud all of the Law, including the blessings and curses.

47. The purpose of these stones was to inform sojourners near Mount Ebal that "this great nation is a wise and understanding people" (Deuteronomy 4:5–6). In other words, these stones demonstrated and witnessed the faith Israel had in the one true God.

48. By being unfaithful to God and not following His edicts, the Israelites could forfeit their land inheritance. Later apostasies caused Israel to lose the land, but God's grace brought them back into the land in preparation for the birth of Christ. Unfortunately, some Christians confuse the Israel of the Bible with the modern nation of Israel and believe that modern Israel is permanently entitled to the land in Palestine (see Deuteronomy 28:15–68). Note particularly the words of verses 36–37 regarding the land.

Deceiving Gibeonites

49. The Gibeonites pretended to be from another country, coming to the Israelites to make a pact. To pull off this ruse, the Gibeonites

loaded down their donkeys, put their goods in worn-out sacks, and even wore old clothing so it would appear they had traveled a great distance. Joshua 9:9–10 addresses the Gibeonites' fear of God. God's Word came to them through outside sources, telling of the Israelites' journey from Egypt and their conquest of the two kings, Sihon and Og. The Gibeonites had also probably heard about Jericho and Ai.

50. The theological dilemma is this: God specifically told the Israelites not to make a treaty with any of the Canaanite nations (Exodus 23:23–24). Yet they did what they were commanded not to do, albeit through deception. The Israelites resolved the matter of whether or not to break their word given to the Gibeonites by allowing them to live among them and serve as their woodcutters and water carriers, thus fulfilling Noah's curse (Genesis 9:25–27).

God's Word for Today

51. Unable to fulfill the Law that God intended His people to do, Christ took the curse of the Law (death) onto Himself and died the death we deserve. From God's very first promise of a Savior (Genesis 3:15), through the promises made to Abraham, Isaac, and Jacob, through the foreshadowing of Christ made through the ancient sacrifices, God points forward to the time of their fulfillment in Jesus Christ. In Him, all of God's promises receive a resounding "Yes!"

Lesson 5

Central Campaign: Part II

Theme verse: *Joshua spoke to the LORD . . . in the sight of Israel, "Sun, stand still at Gibeon."*

Joshua 10:12

Objectives

By the power of the Holy Spirit working through God's Word, we will

- Discover how five Amorite kings plotted against Israel;
- Learn how God delivered another victory;
- See how God responded to Joshua by stopping the sun;
- Rejoice in how God provides a remarkable victory for you and me.

52. In order that God might fulfill His promise to Abraham, He declared war on the nations of Canaan. This war was threefold in nature: (1) It protected God's covenant people from falling victim to the apostasy of the Canaanites; (2) It demonstrated God's superiority over the false gods of the region; and (3) It witnessed God's grace to those who wandered there. God's war cleared the way for the birth of Jesus Christ, who is the Prince of Peace, in the land God promised to Abraham and his descendants. It is through Jesus Christ that "all families of the earth shall be blessed" (Genesis 12:3).

53. The Gibeonite curse also put the Gibeonites in close association with God's covenant community, allowing the Israelites to witness God's grace to them in the hope of these people becoming proselytes.

A Five-King Conspiracy

54. The names of the five kings involved in this conspiracy are Adoni-Zedek, king of Jerusalem; Hoham, king of Hebron; Piram, king of Jarmuth; Japhia, king of Lachish; and Debir, king of Eglon (Joshua 10:3). Take a moment to locate each city on your map.

55. The peoples are the Jebusites, while another name for Jerusalem is Jebus. Adoni-Zedek's reasons for war were that he had heard what the Israelites have done to Jericho and Ai and that the Gibeonites had made a treaty with the Israelites. This treaty concerned him because of the Gibeonites' fighting ability and the number of warriors. Gibeon was larger that Ai (Joshua 10:2). When attacked by the five kings, the Gibeonites responded by asking their Israelite allies to come to their aid (Joshua 10:6).

56. This king was Melchizedek. With the reference from Hebrews telling us that Christ was in the order of Melchizedek, we may safely conclude that Melchizedek was a God-fearing king while Adoni-Zedek was not.

The Lord Strikes Back

57. Several examples appear in our text. First, we have God's reassuring words in 10:8. Second, God hurled large hailstones from the sky, killing several troops. Third, God answered Joshua's prayer that the sun stop in the sky until such time that the rout was complete.

58. A rout occurred under God's direction. In Joshua 10:12–13, we see God stopping the sun in the sky. This event alone, and there are others occurring in this text as well, shows the Israelites that the occupation of Canaan is continually in the Lord's hands.

59. We should trust in the Lord, our God, because all Scripture is His very breath and is useful in teaching, rebuking, correcting, and training us in righteousness (2 Timothy 3:15–17).

60. In the opening of Joshua chapter 10, the five kings are filled with self-confidence. Soon, they will be found slinking into a cave like dogs with their tails between their legs (Joshua 10:16). Their encounter with the Lord's army has caused this change.

61. In Genesis 3:15, Christ is described as crushing the head of Satan. This action denotes Jesus' complete victory over Satan, sin, and death on the cross. Jesus Himself declares His victory over Satan through His cross (John 12:31–32), which the apostle John affirms as well (1 John 3:8b).

62. Each of these kings was put to the sword by Joshua. Their bodies were hung from trees until evening. They were then removed from the trees and tossed into the cave where they were found hiding. Five stone markers covered the entrance to the cave at Makkedah where the five kings were buried.

God's Word for Today

63. By destroying those whose actions warrant death (Law), God preserved His people and cleared a path for the birth of His Son, Jesus Christ (Gospel).

64. The wrath of God was poured out against one man at Calvary's cross, where the Savior of the world willingly went to His death. Sinners such as you and I are pardoned by God and receive eternal life because of Him.

Lesson 6

Northern and Southern Campaigns

Theme verse: *All the cities of those kings, and all their kings, Joshua captured, and struck them with the edge of the sword.*

Joshua 11:12

Objectives

By the power of the Holy Spirit working through God's Word, we will

- Learn about Joshua's prayer life;
- See how the list of conquered cities grows under God's direction;
- Study the significance of the conquest of Hazor;
- Rejoice that God protects His New Testament Church just as He protected His Old Testament Church.

65. A number of verses in our study begin with "the LORD said to Joshua," implying that Joshua had a very intimate relationship with God. The New Testament frequently records Jesus in prayer. The account of both of these men clearly puts the onus on our prayer life and the importance of prayer in our daily walk with God.

66. To date we have studied six memorials: the two following the Jordan River crossing (Joshua 4:8, 20), one over the grave of Achan and his family (7:26), one over the ruins of Ai (8:29), one at Mount Ebal (8:32), and one over the entrance to the cave at Makkedah (10:27). Each memorial stands as a tribute to what God has done on behalf of and through the Israelites in Canaan.

The Southern Campaign

67. The military engagements during the southern campaign total seven, which is God's number of completeness. By setting the number of engagements at seven, the writer of Joshua is telling us that the conquest of the South was complete.

68. The cities whose names were associated with the five kings are Lachish, Eglon, and Hebron. Each of these cities was totally destroyed during the southern campaign and their citizens put to the sword.

69. The city of Lachish was conquered in two days at the Lord's hand.

70. Joshua 10:42–43 tells us that the southern campaign was accomplished during one campaign after which the Israelites returned to their home base at Gilgal.

The Northern Campaign

71. The instigator is Jabin, king of Hazor, who seems to organize his group of local kings after hearing that the Israelites have returned to their base camp.

72. The Lord's plan will be accomplished in twenty-four hours (Joshua 11:6) and calls for Joshua's troops to hamstring the horses, burn the chariots, and complete a surprise attack near the waters of Merom, pursuing them to Greater Sidon, Misrephoth Maim, and into the Valley of Mizpah.

73. Hazor was destroyed because Jabin, king of Hazor, was the leader of this conspiracy. All the other cities were left for Israelite habitation, fulfilling the prophecy that they will live in cities they did not build (Deuteronomy 6:10–11).

74. The Anakites are the descendants of Anak (Numbers 13:28, 33). These men who appeared so formidable during the original trip by the twelve spies were destroyed by the Israelites at Anab, Hebron, and Debir (Joshua 11:21). Matthew 26 contains words that could be applied to the unfaithfulness of ten of the twelve spies Moses sent into Canaan.

75. Spend time reviewing the land conquered by Joshua at the Lord's command.

76. Perhaps the chronicling is purposefully sparse to show at a glance all that the Lord has done.

God's Word for Today

77. The list of those who opposed the New Testament Church include Herod the Great, Herod Antipas (whom Jesus calls "the Fox"), Annas, Caiphas, Pontius Pilate, Jewish religious leaders, and Felix.

78. Romans 8:35–39 states that nothing shall separate us from God's love. We can see that when we look at the list of those who attacked God's Old Testament Church and those who came in opposition to God's New Testament Church. No matter the circumstances, God will accomplish what He desires. In Colossians 2:14–15, we learn that God's Law came against us to condemn us, but Christ took the Law upon Himself and nailed it to the tree. So the Law condemns, but God's grace in Christ Jesus saves.

79. The author of Hebrews teaches us that our strengthening of faith comes through the Gospel and the Sacraments of Baptism and the Lord's Supper.

Lesson 7

Allotting the Transjordan

Theme verse: *With the other half of the tribe of Manasseh the Reubenites and the Gadites received their inheritance, which Moses gave them, beyond the Jordan eastward, as Moses the servant of the LORD gave them.*

Joshua 13:8

Objectives

By the power of the Holy Spirit working through God's Word, we will

- Explore the lands remaining to be conquered;
- Review the area occupied by the Hebrews east of the Jordan;
- Discover why the Levites received no land inheritance;
- Learn that as Christians we receive no land inheritance now but will inherit a new heaven and a new earth at Christ's return.

80. Items for discussion should include: God's promise to guide and direct Joshua (Joshua 1:2–5); God's encouragement of Joshua (1:6); God's promise to exalt Joshua's leadership in the eyes of the Israelites (1:7); God's pronouncement and fulfillment of plans, both societal and military, for Joshua (3:8; 5:2–3; 6:2–5); and God's involvement in military campaigns (e.g., He sent large hailstones and caused the sun to stand still during the battle against the five Amorite kings; 10:11–14). The first twelve chapters of Joshua are filled with God's faithfulness, a faithfulness that permeates this entire book.

81. Answers will vary.

Lands Remaining to Be Taken

82. Lands remaining include (1) the regions of the Philistines and Geshurites from the Shihor River on the east of Egypt to the territory of Ekron on the north; from the south, all of the land of the Canaanites, from Arah of the Sidonians as far as Aphek; the regions of the Amorites; the area of the Gebalites; all of Lebanon to the east, from Baal-gad below Mount Hermon to Lebo-hamath (Joshua 13:1–5).

83. God discloses that He will drive the Sidonians from the land and encourages Joshua to divide the land among the Israelites although the land conquest is incomplete (Joshua 13:6–7).

84. Some believe that the Philistines journeyed from Crete and elsewhere in the Mediterranean Sea area to settle in the land of Canaan.

85. The Hebrew patriarchs familiar with the Philistines included Abraham (Genesis 20:1; 21:32, 34) and Isaac (Genesis 26:1). The most famous Philistine was Goliath, who met his death at the hands of the boy David.

Transjordan Land Assignments

86. The Levites receive offerings made by fire to the Lord (Joshua 13:4). Deuteronomy 18:1–8 provides the specifics of this proviso: the Levites received the shoulder, the jowls, and the inner parts of a sacrificed bull or sheep. They also received the firstfruits of the Israelites' harvested grain, new wine and oil, and the first wool from the sheep shearing. In a subsequent study, we will learn about the cities of refuge and Levitical cities where the Levites may live in locations throughout the Cisjordan and Transjordan.

87. Reuben and Gad were sons of Jacob (later known as Israel, the name ascribed to his descendants) through Leah, while Manasseh was the firstborn son of Joseph. Manasseh and Ephraim were adopted as sons by Jacob (Genesis 48:5). These descendants of Manasseh and Ephraim each received an inheritance in Canaan, thereby allotting two shares for Joseph. Joseph's name is not listed among the names of the twelve tribes for that reason.

God's Word for Today

88. Jesus teaches that we are to depend on God for our existence, just as the ancient Levites did. Throughout this study, you may have noticed how Joshua lives his life dependent on God.

89. Indeed, our lives run parallel to the ancients. In all cases, sin leads to death, but we have received eternal life by the grace of God in Christ. God's Spirit works faith through the Gospel. In the case of the Israelites, they had faith in the coming Messiah to deliver them from sin; in our case, it is faith that this promised Savior is Christ Jesus.

Lesson 8

Allotment at Gilgal

Theme verse: *Surely the land on which your foot has trodden shall be an inheritance for you and your children.*

Joshua 14:9

Objectives

By the power of the Holy Spirit working through God's Word, we will

- Learn why Caleb was given the first choice of land in Canaan;
- Understand the lineage of the twelve tribes of Israel;
- Rejoice as tribes receive the Lord's land inheritance;
- Thank God for the victory of our salvation won by Jesus Christ.

90. We recall Caleb's trust in the Lord because he returned to Moses with a favorable report on the land (Numbers 13:30). His trust is rewarded by God with the promise of land in Canaan (Numbers 14:24). In response to Caleb's faithful service, Joshua allows Caleb to select his land first. Note that apart from Joshua's own selection of land in Canaan, all other property is awarded by the Lord either by drawing lots or through the use of the Urim and Thummim.

91. The lineage of Jacob (renamed Israel by God) is as follows: Reuben through Leah, Jacob's wife; Simeon through Leah; Levi through Leah; Judah through Leah; Dan through Bilhah, Rachel's servant; Naphtali through Bilhah; Gad through Zilpah, Leah's servant; Asher through Zilpah; Issachar through Leah; Zebulon through Leah; and Joseph and Benjamin through Rachel. You might recall that Joseph's sons bear the names of two tribes, Manasseh and Ephraim. While Joseph's name is not mentioned, his tribe carries on through his

two sons. Since the Levites receive no land inheritance, the count of the tribes remains at twelve.

Caleb's Request

92. Nine and a half tribes receive their allotted land in Canaan, while the Levites receive only towns to live with adjoining pasture lands for their flocks and herds.

93. A. Joshua 14:7
B. Joshua 14:12–14; Deuteronomy 1:36
C. Joshua 14:10–11
D. Joshua 14:8
E. Joshua 14:13

94. Caleb is of the tribe of Judah, and these men approached Joshua to offer their support of Caleb's land request.

Judah's Allotment

95. Jacob prophesies the coming kings of Israel fulfilled in David and ultimately fulfilled in Jesus Christ. In Christ's lineage outlined in Matthew, we discover that Judah is his ancestor, fulfilling Jacob's prophecy.

96. Judah's tribe could not drive out the Jebusites living in Jerusalem (Joshua 15:63). That won't happen until the time of King David (2 Samuel 6–10).

97. Othniel becomes Caleb's son-in-law by defeating the city of Kiriath Sepher. Since true blessings come from the Lord, we see Achsah's faith in her request that Caleb bless her.

Ephraim and Manasseh's Allotment

98. Joshua is of the tribe of Ephraim. Joshua 16:10 presents a recurring theme that the tribes of Israel never drove the inhabitants of Canaan from their land as God had commanded.

99. The five daughters of Zelophehad requested their land. Moses had previously ruled in their favor. The descendants of Joseph requested that the land of their inheritance be enlarged. These descendants are from the tribes of Ephraim and Manasseh and their fellow tribesman, therefore, is Joshua. Joshua tells his fellow tribesmen that they will receive but one allotment and that if they want more land

they must clear the forested country in their allotment. These tribes were unable to drive the Canaanites from their territory (Joshua 17:12).

God's Word for Today

100. The common thread is that the Israelites never drove the Canaanites from their land. The Israelites were unable to drive out the Canaanites because their faith in God was weak. They no longer trusted that God would do all He had promised, including leading them to victory over the Canaanites (Deuteronomy 28:1–14). Faith comes from the Holy Spirit (1 Corinthians 12:3) through God's Word. Therefore, we participate in the means of grace, the Gospel and the Sacraments of Baptism and Holy Communion.

101. 1 Corinthians 15:56–57 says our victory comes through God who grants it through His Son, Jesus Christ. Romans 7:24–25 says that as wretched, sinful human beings, our salvation comes only through the atoning death of Jesus Christ.

Lesson 9

The Allotment at Shiloh

Theme verse: *The land lay subdued before them. There remained among the people of Israel seven tribes whose inheritance had not yet been apportioned.*

Joshua 18:1–2

Objectives

By the power of the Holy Spirit working through God's Word, we will

- Witness the surveying of the land of Canaan;
- Learn of God's land allotment to the remaining seven tribes;
- Discover the land the Israelites gave Joshua;
- Apply Joshua's warning in Joshua 18:3 to our own lives.

102. Scholars continue to debate the reason for the move, but a probable explanation for it is that Shiloh is centrally located for each tribe to go and worship there.

103. First, the land must be taken by force from its Canaanite occupants. After that feat is accomplished, the Israelites may occupy Canaanite cities, making them their dwelling place.

Benjamin's Allotment

104. Joshua's plan involved sending three men from each of the remaining tribes into the land. Their assignment was to survey the territory and provide Joshua with a description. Once this task was completed, Joshua would draw lots for the land in the presence of the Lord, in the Tent of Meeting, and in the presence of Eleazar, the high priest.

105. The tribe received the city of Jericho, which was not to be rebuilt, and Jerusalem. The ravenous Benjamite king is Saul, the first king of Israel.

Simeon and Zebulun's Allotment

106. At Beersheba, Abraham made a treaty with the Philistine king Abimelech. Did you notice that the Holy Spirit has worked faith in Abimelech for he tells Abraham that he knows God is with him (Genesis 21:22)?

107. The young man referred to by the Gospel writer is Jesus of Nazareth.

Issachar and Asher's Allotment

108. Jacob describes his son Issachar as a "strong donkey crouching between the sheepfolds" (Genesis 49:14).

109. By failing to drive out the inhabitants of the land, the tribe of Asher repeats a common theme of those living in Canaan.

Naphtali and Dan's Allotment

110. Matthew teaches that the city Jesus often visited during his earthly ministry is the city of Capernaum.

111. The Danites had difficulty conquering the land given to them, so they headed north and conquered the city of Leshem and settled there. (Take time to locate Leshem on your map.) Jacob describes Dan as "a serpent in the way," in other words, cunning and sly (Genesis 49:17). Josephus, a first-century AD Jewish historian, describes the Danites as slothful men who neglected God and who ultimately contaminated themselves with Canaanite practices.

Joshua's Allotment

112. Joshua was given the city of Timnath Serah, which was found in the hill country of the land allotted to Ephraim. The words of Psalm 149:14–16 show us a man who served his people faithfully by "keeping them close to his heart." As we have seen throughout this study, Joshua put God first and then all others ahead of himself and was certainly a sterling example of a man of God.

God's Word for Today

113. In Joshua 18:3, we see that the seven remaining tribes are dragging their feet in claiming their land inheritance. Joshua chides them with the words, "How long will you wait before you begin to take possession?" These words are an example of Law with its condemning and accusing nature. The application of the Gospel comes from Joshua's reminder that God will keep His promise and provide this land for their inheritance.

114. As exemplified through the life of Joshua and his words in Joshua 18:3, we learn that we should be bold in our trust of the Lord. The words of Philippians 1:6 are often spoken after the Sacrament of Baptism. God begins each work in us, makes us bold, and calls us into His service through the Holy Spirit. Since these works we do are begun by God, we should be confident that He will complete these works to His glory.

Lesson 10

Levitical Cities

Theme verse: *Thus the LORD gave to Israel all the land that He swore to give to their fathers. And they took possession of it, and they settled there.*

Joshua 21:43

Objectives

By the power of the Holy Spirit working through God's Word, we will

- Discover the purpose behind God's cities of refuge;
- Appreciate why God apportioned Levitical cities throughout Israel;
- Understand the role the Kohathites played in the Levitical priesthood;
- Grow in appreciation of the blessing derived from Levi's curse.

115. The Levites were God's Old Testament priests who taught the Israelites God's Word. A select group that descended directly through Aaron were put in charge of conducting the Divine Service. They had to learn its system of sacrifices and distinguish between what was clean and unclean (Leviticus 10:8–11).

116. Cities of refuge were six cities given to the Levites as safe havens for someone who accidentally killed another and committed unintentional homicide. Of these six cities, three were located east of the Jordan and three west of the Jordan.

Cities of Refuge

117. The avenger of blood was a blood relative of a murdered individual. He was responsible for avenging the victim by killing the person who committed the murder. Although the avenger of blood was guilty of murder under the Law, he was not held responsible. God's command to Noah was that should one person murder another, the life of the murderer should likewise be forfeit. Genesis 9:6 teaches that within God's system of justice, capital punishment is permitted. However, capital punishment should never be taken lightly, because the death of another individual is always a serious matter.

118. Numbers 35:22–23 speaks about someone who killed another unintentionally by shoving or throwing something at him or who accidentally drops a stone on him. Deuteronomy 19:5 discusses someone who commits an unintentional killing when an axe head accidentally flies off and strikes and kills him. These verses point out only two examples of unintentional murder, but others were possible under Jewish law, with each decided by the Levites living in the city of refuge.

119. A murderer could flee to a city of refuge if he maintained his murder was accidental. He had to stand at the city gate and plead his case before the Levites who were the city elders. They could either allow the man to enter or turn him away. If an avenger of blood arrived at the city gates, the Levites must protect the accused until they could hold a trial to determine the accused's guilt or innocence. Scholars have haggled over the word *and* found in Joshua 20:6 as it applies here. Some believe the word *or* should take its place, giving the murderer but one condition to meet: either he stands trial or he waits until the high priest dies before returning home. Numbers 35:24–25 states that both conditions, the trial and the death of the high priest, must be met before the person who killed unintentionally could return home. Based on the location of each city of refuge, it appears that these cities could be reached easily by someone walking.

120. David repented of his sin before God and received His forgiveness. Keep in mind that David's sin did not go without temporal consequences, because the Lord claimed David's son by Bathsheba (2 Samuel 12:14–15). God desires that we repent and seek His forgiveness just as David did.

Levitical Cities

121. The allotment of Levitical cities occurred at Shiloh (Joshua 21:1–2).

122. The Kohathite cites were all located near Jerusalem, making their service at God's temple easily accessible because of God's plan of drawing of lots.

123. Through Jacob's curse, the Levites were scattered throughout Canaan. God might scatter the Levites to make it possible for each tribe to have a teacher of the Law within their boundaries. Such a scattering allowed the Levites to fulfill their duties to teach the Israelites, a duty God assigned them (Leviticus 10:8–11).

124. The words of Joshua 21:43–45 provide the Israelites of this and subsequent generations with the knowledge that it is God who provided them with their land inheritance, giving them rest in His time. Verse 45 is especially important. Joshua notes that God has fulfilled all of His promises. These words serve as a vivid reminder of what God has provided. Therefore, the Israelites should refer to this passage in difficult times instead of placing their confidence in themselves. The apostle John records the purpose of his Gospel quite pointedly in John 20:31. His Gospel was written that we may believe in Jesus Christ and have eternal life. The writer of Joshua makes the same point about believing in Joshua 21:45. Because the land distribution is completed, God has kept His promises found in Genesis 12:2–3. He promised to make Abraham's family into a great nation that will receive His blessing. He also promised to make Abraham's name great because of its association with God's covenant people who are now living in the land of promise. God has blessed Abraham through this gift of land, and those who bless Abraham's descendents are blessed in return (e.g., Rahab and the Gibeonites), and those who curse Abraham's descendants are cursed (e.g., the five Amorites kings). With the Israelites in the land, the road is now paved for God to fulfill the most important part of His promise: the deliverance of His people from their sin through His precious Son, Jesus Christ.

God's Word for Today

125. One result of Levi's curse was that God's priestly order was scattered throughout Canaan. Because of that, God's people were taught God's Word, and although some later fell away, others

remained as a faithful remnant to provide the nucleus through which God provided the Savior of the World.

126. Samuel reminds us that God is our refuge. The Romans and Galatians texts instruct us that because of the redeeming work of Jesus Christ we are made heirs of Abraham and inheritors of God's promises. We should recall these promises each time we witness a Baptism or partake in the Holy Eucharist.

Lesson 11

God's Heirs Respond

Theme verse: *The LORD has driven out before you great and strong nations.*

Joshua 23:9

Objectives

By the power of the Holy Spirit working through God's Word, we will

- Rejoice as Joshua sends the Transjordan troops home;
- Contemplate Joshua's steadfast faith;
- Mourn the loss of Joshua, son of Nun, the servant of the Lord;
- Discover the commonality between God's Old and New Testament Church.

Transjordan Troops Released

127. Transjordan troops did all that Joshua has requested of them, thereby fulfilling their vows originally made to Moses. The Transjordan troops did not return empty-handed. They carried with them the booty accumulated through years of fighting—livestock, silver and gold, bronze and iron, and clothing—knowing they are to share with their brothers when they return home. Their dismissal took place at Shiloh, the seat of Israelite worship prior to Jerusalem (Joshua 22:22). Did you notice the three parts to this important address? First, Joshua compliments his troops (Joshua 22:2–4); second, Joshua exhorts his troops (v. 5); and, finally, Joshua blesses them before sending them home (vv. 6–8).

128. Joshua exhorts his troops to remain faithful to God and serve Him with all their hearts and souls. This phrase is remarkably similar to the words of Jesus, our New Testament Joshua, in Matthew 22:37. It

is echoed throughout the other Synoptic Gospels and repeated in Colossians (Mark 12:30, 33; Luke 10:27; Colossians 3:23).

129. After leaving Shiloh, the Transjordan troops erected an altar at Geliloth near the Jordan River. To resolve the conflict arising from the construction of a second altar (the first is now at the Tent of Meeting in Shiloh), Joshua sends Phinehas, son of the high priest, as well as ten other men, one from each of the ten tribes. The conflict dissipates after the Transjordan tribes convince Phinehas that the new altar was erected only as a reminder of what God has done. It was not intended as a second worship site. This conflict presents an example of conflict resolution within the Church. Believers are to confront each other in love. Christian men and women should seek a peaceful resolution to conflict as demonstrated in Joshua and in Matthew 18. Again, with these texts we see a great similarity between Joshua of the Old Testament and Jesus in the New Testament.

Joshua's Second Farewell

130. Joshua's second farewell address is delivered to the elders, leaders, judges, and officials who are looking out for the best interests of the Israelites. We may conclude that this address is to these men, because we read that Joshua gathered all the tribes at Shechem (Joshua 24:1). No location is named for this speech, but likely places are at Shiloh, at Joshua's home in Timnath-serah, or at Shechem, which is the location of Joshua's final sermon. It is important that the men gathered before Joshua hear this message as a reminder of their status as leaders of the Israelites. Joshua wants the image of God's faithfulness emblazoned on their hearts.

131. There are three references to God's faithfulness (Joshua 23:3–5). The "I" Joshua uses in these verses is not a selfish "Look what I did" but an implied "Through the help of the Lord." Discuss the difference.

132. To remain holy in God's sight the Israelites must (1) not associate with the Canaanites, (2) not invoke the name of their gods, (3) not swear by these false gods, and 4) not serve them or bow down before them. Such practices stand in violation of the first two commandments (Exodus 20:3–7). Consequences for such despicable practices are chronicled in Joshua 23:12–16. A violation of God's commands will result in God's removing of His hand of grace. God cannot dwell among an unholy people. (See Leviticus 26:14–33, and

be sure to notice how many times God willingly calls His people back to Him, providing a solid example of God's abundant grace.)

133. Yes. In order for God to dwell with them and for them to share in His holiness, they must keep His commands. Failure to do so disconnects God's people from His presence, which causes severe consequences. Thankfully, you and I are made right in our relationship with God through the blood of Christ (Hebrews 9:14).

Covenant Renewal and a Third Farewell

134. Joshua's account of God's faithfulness includes the story of Abraham, his son Isaac, and grandsons Jacob and Esau; Moses, Aaron, and the Red Sea deliverance; the defeat of the Transjordan kings; the Jordan River crossing and victory at Jericho; subsequent victories over the Canaanites and their various tribes; and a restatement of their land allotment.

135. God warns His people not to forsake the Lord their God. Failure to do so will mean a withdrawal of God's grace, leading to disaster and, ultimately, to a forfeiture of the Israelites' land inheritance. These warnings are very similar to the blessings and curses Moses presents in Deuteronomy 28 and 29.

136. The Israelites pledged to remain faithful to God (Joshua 24:16–18; 21–24). A large stone memorial was erected "under the terebinth that was by the sanctuary of the LORD" (Joshua 24:26). In all, seven memorials are constructed as visual reminders of God's faithfulness. The memorial detailed here as being "under the terebinth" may or may not be the same tree spoken of at the time of Abraham (Genesis 12:6). If this is the same tree, what a beautiful symmetry is achieved with the erection of this memorial, because God closes the loop between His promises to Abraham and their fulfillment at the time of Joshua.

137. The burials of Joshua and Eleazar, the high priest, are noted in this text. Additionally, we learn of the burial of Joseph's bones, which the Israelites carried out of Egypt during the Exodus. The writer of Joshua refers to him as "the servant of the LORD" (Joshua 24:29), revealing Joshua's faithfulness in carrying out everything the Lord asked of him. Joseph was also a man of God who trusted in all of God's promises, a man whom God brought back to Canaan so that he might be buried there.

God's Word for Today

138. The common thread of our belief is in the Messiah who came to deliver the world from its sin. God had promised Him to Adam and Eve. The Old Testament believers looked forward to His coming, while New Testament believers give thanks for Jesus coming. Romans 4:20–24 can easily apply to Joshua, though the words were originally spoken of Abraham: "No distrust made him waver concerning the promise of God, but he grew strong in his faith as he gave glory to God, fully convinced that God was able to do what He had promised" (Romans 4:20–21). All of God's promises are "Yes" in Christ who continues to come to us through His Word and Sacraments.

CPSIA information can be obtained
at www.ICGtesting.com
Printed in the USA
FSOW04n0948171017
40000FS